RA

ALSO BY ROY CONYERS NESBIT

Woe to the Unwary
Torpedo Airmen
The Strike Wings
Target: Hitler's Oil (with Ron C. Cooke)
Arctic Airmen (with Ernest Schofield)
Failed to Return
An Illustrated History of the RAF
RAF Records in the PRO (with Simon Fowler, Peter Elliott and Christina Goulter)
The Armed Rovers
The RAF in Camera 1903–1939
Eyes of the RAF

THE RAF
IN CAMERA

ARCHIVE PHOTOGRAPHS FROM THE PUBLIC RECORD OFFICE
AND THE MINISTRY OF DEFENCE

1939–1945

ROY CONYERS NESBIT

Assisted by Oliver Hoare

SUTTON PUBLISHING LIMITED
IN ASSOCIATION WITH THE PUBLIC RECORD OFFICE

First published in the United Kingdom in 1996 by
Alan Sutton Publishing Ltd, an imprint of Sutton Publishing Limited
Phoenix Mill · Thrupp · Stroud · Gloucestershire
in association with the Public Record Office

Paperback edition first published 1997

British Library Cataloguing in Publication Data

A catalogue record for this book is available from the British Library.

ISBN 0-7509-1521-8

™ ALAN SUTTON™ and SUTTON™ are the
trade marks of Sutton Publishing Limited

Typeset in 11/15pt Baskerville.
Typesetting and origination by
Sutton Publishing Limited.
Printed in Great Britain by
WBC, Bridgend, Mid Glam.

CONTENTS

Fire practice as part of air raid precautions at the Public Record Office in Chancery Lane, London.
PRO ref: PRO 50/59

INTRODUCTION

For many years numerous photographs relating to the activities of the RAF have remained unrecorded in hundreds of documents in the Public Record Office (PRO), at Kew. Another large collection is housed in the Ministry of Defence in London. This series of three volumes is intended to bring representative photographs of the two collections to the notice of the general public. The volumes are not intended to provide a comprehensive history of the RAF and its predecessors, but they may give some indication of the huge numbers of photographs that are available.

In all cases the reference numbers of the photographs appear underneath the captions. The photographs at the PRO are not housed separately but the originals of each may be seen within their relevant documents by visitors who obtain readers' tickets and then request the numbers on computer terminals in the Reference Room. However, it should be noted that documents at the PRO are not normally available for public scrutiny until they are thirty years old, and the same stipulation applies to photographs.

A catalogue of many photographs of all types at the PRO has been built up and is available in the Reference Room, but at the time of writing (1995) this is by no means complete. A description of the contents of this catalogue is contained in PRO Records Information leaflet 90. Copies of RAF photographs, or any others found by readers, may be purchased via the Reprographic Ordering Section. Details such as choice of process and scale of charges are set out in PRO General Information leaflet 19. Copies of photographs are available for commercial reproduction from the PRO Image Library, telephone 0181-392-5255. Prices will be given on request.

The photographic prints relating to the RAF housed at the Ministry of Defence are not available for public inspection. The main purpose of this collection is to provide information to the RAF and various Government departments, and not to the general public. However, readers may write to the central library where negatives are held if they wish to purchase copies of the photographs contained in these volumes or enquire about others. This is CS(Photography)P, Ministry of Defence, Court 9 Basement, King Charles

Street, London SW1A 2AH, with whom any purchasing arrangements may be made. At present this enormous collection covers the period from the very early days of the RAF and its predecessors up to the Gulf War of 1991.

All the photographs in these three volumes are Crown Copyright. Guidelines for those who propose to reproduce photographs are set out in PRO General Information leaflet 15, and the same guidelines also apply to any photographs purchased from the Ministry of Defence.

This volume is the second of the series of three, and covers the Second World War from September 1939 to August 1945. It includes the Battle of France, the Battle of Britain and the operations of Bomber Command, Fighter Command, Coastal Command and the 2nd Tactical Air Force, as well as some of the other Commands at home. Further afield, there are photographs taken in North Africa, the Middle East, Italy and the Far East. However, there is a far wider selection of photographs available from the RAF's activities in Northern Europe than in more distant theatres, and the book reflects this bias. The choice of photographs also depended partly on their clarity.

The captions underneath these photographs originated from the documents in which they were located in the PRO or the brief captions available in the Ministry of Defence. This information was supplemented by a considerable amount of research in other documents in the PRO or reliable books of reference. Readers who wish to carry out similar research are recommended to purchase a copy of PRO Readers' Guide No. 8 *RAF Records in the PRO* by Simon Fowler, Peter Elliott, Roy Conyers Nesbit and Christina Goulter (PRO Publications 1994), available from the PRO shop at the Public Record Office, Ruskin Avenue, Kew, Richmond, Surrey TW9 4DU. This guide also includes an appendix listing other sources of RAF photographs within Great Britain.

Note PRO leaflets are constantly being updated and their reference numbers are therefore liable to change from time to time.

ACKNOWLEDGEMENTS

I should like to express my gratitude to Simon Fowler and Oliver Hoare of the PRO for their painstaking help in hunting for suitable photographs. Similarly, I am most grateful to Group Captain Ian Madelin RAF (Ret'd) and Squadron Leader Peter Singleton RAF (Ret'd) of the Air Historical Branch (RAF), Ministry of Defence, for permission to include many official photographs housed in the MoD, as well as to Bill Hunt of the Whitehall Library for reproducing the MoD prints and Mark Laing of Indusfoto for reproducing the PRO prints. My thanks for researching the material for captions are also due to Richard Riding and Michael Oakey of *Aeroplane Monthly*, as well as Rick Chapman of the German aviation magazine *Jet & Prop*. I am extremely grateful to Squadron Leader Dudley Cowderoy RAFVR and Roger Hayward for their work in checking and correcting the captions. Any errors which remain after this expertise are my own responsibility.

PHONEY AND REAL WAR

One of the trades open to recruits in the WAAF was that of Group 5 'balloon-parachute hand'. After training, the airwomen were posted to a site, where they took over the function hitherto carried out by airmen, as can be seen from this publicity photograph of WAAF personnel handling cables when raising a balloon.

PRO ref: INF 2/45

After releasing the cables, the airwomen stood by to steady the balloon.

PRO ref: INF 2/45

At 03.15 hours on 6 December 1939, Heinkel Hell5 radio code S4+BL of *3.Küstenfliegergruppe 506* based at Sylt came down in the sea off Sheringham in Norfolk. It had hit a mast of the 'Chain Home' radar station at West Beckham and then narrowly missed a gas holder when flying out of control. All three crew members, *Oberleutnant zur See* W. Wodtke, *Oberfeldwebel* E. Rödel and *Oberfeldwebel* K. Ullmann were killed. The wreckage of the aircraft became visible when the tide receded; it was broken in two and both engines were missing.

PRO ref: AIR 28/75

The body of the air observer, *Oberfeldwebel* Emil Rödel, aged 29, was washed ashore. His uniform and flying boots were removed and photographed.

PRO ref: AIR 28/75

Oberfeldwebel Emil Rödel was buried with full military honours at Great Bircham churchyard on 9 December 1939. His coffin was covered with the German national flag, and six RAF sergeants carried out the duties of pall bearers. The personnel attending the funeral were from RAF Bircham Newton.

PRO ref: AIR 28/75

Airmen guarding Fairey Battles of the RAF's Air Striking Force at an airfield in France during an early stage of the war. Five squadrons equipped with these aircraft were almost wiped out when they made a series of attacks against the advancing Wehrmacht after the Blitzkrieg began on 10 May 1940. Thereafter, most of the remaining aircraft were employed on training duties.

MoD ref: C170

A squadron leader at Wing Headquarters in France studying photographs taken by reconnaissance aircraft over Germany. The device behind the binoculars on his desk is a stereoscopic viewer with two magnifying lenses. When two photographs, taken vertically and overlapping each other by 60 per cent, were slid under the viewer, objects seemed to stand up and give a startling third dimension. Interpretation of aerial photographs, mostly taken by high-altitude Spitfires and Mosquitos, became one of the major intelligence successes in the Second World War. Some interpreters were academics who specialized in this field and volunteered for the service. Others were WAAF officers, who soon excelled as photo-interpreters.

MoD ref: C127

(*Opposite, top*) Mary Cooper and Dora Lang, pilots of the Air Transport Auxiliary (ATA), photographed beside an Avro Anson. The ATA was a civilian organization formed in February 1940 and administered by the British Airways Corporation. The main function of the men and women pilots was ferrying new aircraft from factories to RAF stations, thus relieving the RAF of the task. A number of these pilots lost their lives from various causes before the ATA was wound up in November 1945.

MoD ref: CH8943

(*Opposite, bottom*) An F24 camera being handed to the air observer of a Bristol Blenheim. Some of these aircraft were employed on daylight photo-reconnaissance over Germany in the early days of the war but they proved easy prey for German fighters and only minor results were achieved. Far better results were gained by unarmed Spitfire Is fitted with cameras, known at first as the Special Survey Flight and later as 212 Squadron.

MoD ref: C116

This fighter pilot, equipped with parachute and oxygen mask, going aboard his Hurricane I of 73 Squadron, was photographed in France during the 'Phoney War' when the squadron formed part of the Air Component of the British Expeditionary Force. Ten Hurricane squadrons flew with the Force after the Wehrmacht attacked in the west on 10 May 1940. These fighters took a heavy toll of the Luftwaffe but they fought against heavy odds and 195 of their number were destroyed, damaged or rendered unserviceable. Only sixty-six were flown back to England when the French airfields became untenable, to continue the fight from home bases.

MoD ref: C186

Part of the armada of 299 British warships and 420 other vessels, including little ships manned by volunteers, which evacuated 335,490 officers and men from Dunkirk between 27 May and 4 June 1940.

PRO ref: AIR 35/329

Fires at Dunkirk, to where the British Expeditionary Force and elements of the French and Belgian armies began a fighting retreat on 26 May 1940, relentlessly pursued by German Panzers.

PRO ref: AIR 35/329

A pilot of 19 Squadron, which was equipped with Spitfire Is and based at Hornchurch in Essex, photographed on 30 May 1940 while walking past the nose of a Hurricane.

MoD ref: CH165

THE BATTLE OF BRITAIN

This photograph of a pilot clambering out of a Spitfire was taken in October 1940. The Battle of Britain began on 10 July 1940 and lasted until 12 October (the day when Hitler postponed his planned invasion of Britain), although some daylight raids continued until the end of that month. In later years 'Battle of Britain Day' was celebrated on 15 September, the day on which Winston Churchill declared 'The Royal Air Force cut to rags and tatters separate waves of murderous assault upon the civilian population of their native land'. It was reported that 185 enemy aircraft were shot down on that day, although post-war research indicated that the true figure was 60.

VO or Ya = 266 or 616 Sa   MoD ref: CH1358

(*Opposite*) The Filter Room at Fighter Command's headquarters at Bentley Priory in Middlesex. This underground block was opened on 9 March 1940 and became known as 'the hole'. The plotters placed counters representing approaching enemy aircraft formations, including altitude and suggested strength, on the table as reports came in from various radar stations. On the right, outside the photograph, tellers watched progress and informed the Operations Room next door, where the raiders were plotted from reports which came in from Observer Corps posts after the enemy had crossed the coast. The Operations Room issued orders to defending RAF stations, which vectored their aircraft on to the enemy aircraft.

MoD ref: X26387

The Receiver Room in one of the 'Chain Home' radar stations, twenty-two of which were situated on the coastline. The photograph shows the RF8 RX receiver on the left, with the operator in front of the radar tube display. On the right, in front of the console, a WAAF signals corporal is passing messages by phone and Morse code, while the signals aircraftman next to her is keeping a log of events. The man next to him is receiving the signals from the radar operator opposite and placing them on a plotting table. The work of these stations in identifying approaching formations of enemy aircraft, coupled with the rapid sifting of information, was crucial to the RAF's victory in the Battle of Britain.

MoD ref: X60981

(*Opposite*) The Royal Observer Corps stemmed from a voluntary organization which was set up in 1914 to report to the Admiralty any aircraft or airships seen within 60 miles of London. Between the wars, observer posts were built throughout England, Scotland and Wales, and in August 1939 the men were mobilized under the RAF's Fighter Command. Some 10,000 civilian volunteers in the Observer Corps took over the duties of reporting numbers of enemy aircraft, with altitude and speed, once they had crossed the coastline. The equipment of each post consisted of a primitive theodolite, binoculars and a telephone. Their work in the Battle of Britain was so valuable that King George VI conferred the title 'Royal' on the Corps.

MoD ref: CH13901

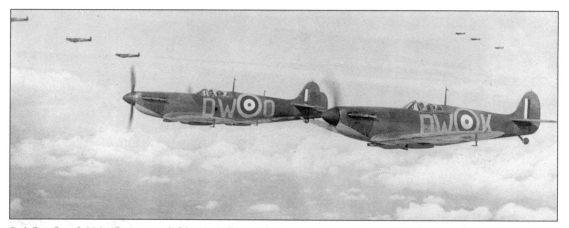

Spitfire Is of 610 (County of Chester) Squadron on patrol in July 1940 from their base at Biggin Hill in Kent.

MoD ref: CH170

Spitfire pilots of 609 (West Riding) Squadron photographed at Warmwell in Dorset in July 1940, beside the tent which served as their crewroom. Standing, left to right: Pilot Officer E.Q. Tobin* (American), Pilot Officer P. Ostaszeski-Ostoje (Polish), Flying Officer H.McD. Goodwin*, Flying Officer A.R. Edge, Pilot Officer M.J. Appleby, Flight Lieutenant F.J. Howell, Squadron Leader H.S. Darley, Flight Lieutenant J.H.G. McArthur, Sergeant A.N. Feary*, Pilot Officer T. Nowierski (Polish), Pilot Officer C.N. Overton. Front, left to right: Pilot Officer M.E. Staples*, Pilot Officer D.M. Crook*, Pilot Officer R.F.G. Millar* (Australian).
(*Killed in action during the war.)

PRO ref: AIR 4/21

Spitfire I, serial P9322, flown by Pilot Officer David M. Crook of 609 Squadron, being rearmed at Warmwell after an air battle on 9 July 1940, with an airman putting a new oxygen bottle into the cockpit. *damaged by Bf109 25 VIII.1940; crashed Cardiff 15.IX.42*

PRO ref: AIR 4/21

Hurricane I serial P3886 being serviced. This aircraft was taken on charge by 601 (County of London) Squadron at Tangmere in Sussex on 12 July 1940. It remained on the strength of the squadron throughout the Battle of Britain, but was passed to No. 50 Maintenance Unit on 9 December 1940. It later served with other squadrons and units, and its long career lasted until it was struck off charge in India on 28 September 1944.

MoD ref: CH1638

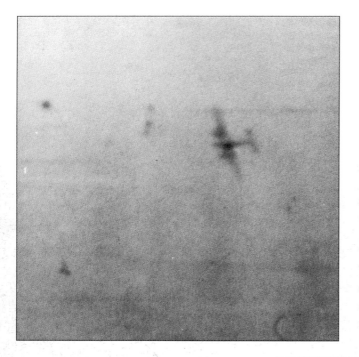

A Messerschmitt Bf110 in the gunsight of Spitfire I, serial N3024, flown by Pilot Officer David M. Crook from Warmwell on 12 August 1940, taken from his camera gun. The enemy aircraft was shot down but during the air battle Crook dived so steeply that the wings of his aircraft were damaged and had to be repaired.

PRO ref: AIR 4/21

Three Spitfire pilots of 609 Squadron at readiness between sorties when operating from Northolt in September 1940. Left to right: Pilot Officer Vernon C. 'Shorty' Keough (American), Pilot Officer Geoffrey N. Gaunt, Pilot Officer David M. Crook. None of these pilots survived the war. Gaunt was killed a few days later, on 15 September, during an air battle over London. Keough transferred to 71 Squadron on 26 September (the first 'Eagle' squadron manned by American personnel to be formed in the RAF) but lost his life on 15 February 1941 on convoy duties from Finningley in Yorkshire, when his Hurricane I, serial V7606, dived unexpectedly into the sea north of Skegness. Crook survived until 18 December 1944 when he was converting onto photo-reconnaissance aircraft with No. 8 Operational Training Unit at Dyce in Aberdeenshire; his Spitfire PR XI, serial EN602, dived into the water north of his station during a high-level exercise, and only parts of his clothing were recovered.

PRO ref: AIR 4/21

Rearming and refuelling a Spitfire during the Battle of Britain; the covers over the leading edges of the wings demonstrate that the eight Browning .303 inch machine-guns had been fired. The squadron letters are only partially visible in this photograph and may be QV, those of 19 Squadron which was based at Fowlmere in Cambridgeshire for much of the period.

MoD ref: CH1367

LZ-K X4170 66 SQUADRON, COLTISHALL.
a/c. of R. OXSPRING
      s/dn 25.x.1940
(other photos in the same sequence give the letters — see A. PRICE SPITFIRE AT WAR.

Hurricane Is, serials P3059 and P3208, of 501 (County of Gloucester) Squadron taking off from Gravesend in Kent on 15 August 1940, at the height of the Battle of Britain. Both these aircraft were lost three days later.

MoD ref: H1495

A bomb disposal officer at work on a German SC250 bomb, beside a crashed German aircraft. The weight of the bomb was 250kg.

PRO ref: AIR 37/1441

(*Opposite, top*) Armourers photographed in October 1940 while at work on Hurricane I, serial L1926, of 312 Squadron at Speke in Lancashire, where the squadron was engaged on defending Merseyside. This squadron was one of two Czechoslovakian fighter squadrons which were operational during the Battle of Britain. The other was 310 Squadron, based at Duxford in Cambridgeshire and also equipped with Hurricanes. The machine in this photograph enjoyed a long life, for it was transferred to the training role and eventually 'struck off charge' in 1944.

MoD ref: CH1434

(*Opposite, bottom*) The elliptical wing is well illustrated in this photograph of a Spitfire IIA of 19 Squadron, taken at Fowlmere in Cambridgeshire in October 1940.

MoD ref: CH1458

A concentration of German barges at Boulogne, ready for an invasion of Britain in the summer of 1940.

PRO ref: AIR 14/3668

Typical German barges on the Rhine. They varied in length from 100 to 300 feet, and the largest had a displacement of 3,000 tons.

PRO ref: AIR 14/3668

A mosaic built up from several overlapping vertical photographs of Rotterdam, taken in September 1940. The photo-interpreters were able to pick out an ominous concentration of about 650 barges, ready for an invasion of Britain. Of these, most were in the Mallegat and the Cude Plantage, with about 110 in the Coolhaven.

PRO ref: AIR 14/3668

This concentration of German invasion barges assembled at Dunkirk was photographed on 19 September 1940 from 3,100 feet by Blenheim IV, serial T2032, of 82 Squadron, flown by Pilot Officer Metcalfe. Twelve Blenheims of this squadron took off from Bodney in Norfolk for bombing and photo-reconnaissance of the port. Eleven turned back since there was no cloud cover but Metcalfe continued alone and carried out an attack, returning with his aircraft holed by flak.

PRO ref: AIR 34/741

(*Opposite*) Squadron Leader A.G. 'Sailor' Malan, a South African serving in the RAF, was one of the most celebrated fighter pilots in the Battle of Britain. He earned his first DFC for operations over Dunkirk and then a DSO after taking over command of 74 Squadron, equipped with Spitfires, in August 1940. A bar to his DFC followed in 1940 and then a bar to his DSO in 1941 for operations over France. He commanded an RAF station and then a wing of the 2nd Tactical Air Force. He retired from the RAF in 1946 with the rank of group captain and returned to South Africa, where he died in 1963 at the age of 52.

MoD ref: CH1875

Group Captain Douglas R.S. Bader (left), photographed on 16 July 1961 at the unveiling of a statue to Viscount Trenchard on Victoria Embankment Gardens. He was commissioned in the RAF in 1930 but invalided out the following year after losing both legs in a flying accident. However, he managed to rejoin the RAF in November 1939. He fought over Dunkirk during the Battle of France and then commanded 242 (Canadian) Squadron, equipped with Hurricanes, during the Battle of Britain. He was captured by the Germans after a collision with an enemy aircraft over France on 9 August 1941 and remained a PoW for most of the remainder of the war. He was awarded a CBE, the DSO and bar, the DFC and bar, the Légion d'Honneur and the Croix de Guerre, and was Mentioned in Despatches three times. He was knighted in 1976 and died on 4 September 1982.

PRO ref: AIR 2/16130

NORTH AFRICA AND THE MED

These Gloster Gladiators of K Flight, 112 Squadron, were based at Helwan in Egypt but detached to Wadi Halfa in the Sudan in June 1940. The detachment was later absorbed by 14 Squadron at Port Sudan and engaged on operations against the Italians in Eritrea.

PRO ref: AIR 27/1503

The Curtiss Tomahawk IIB single-seat fighter entered service with 250 Squadron at Aqir in Palestine in April 1941. The squadron moved to the Western Desert in the following month, as shown in this photograph, and began ground-attack and tactical reconnaissance operations against the Italians.

PRO ref: AIR 27/1503

One of several Fiat G.50 Freccia single-seat fighters damaged or burnt out on the airfield of Sidi Rezegh, south-east of Tobruk. This airfield changed hands several times in the desert war, first being occupied by the British in January 1941. An RAF Hurricane can be seen on the right.

MoD ref: CM1825

The Italian cruiser *San Giorgio* of 9,232 tons was crippled in Tobruk harbour during an RAF raid on 12 June 1940, two days after Italy entered the war. She was then beached and employed as a floating battery, but finally blown up by the Italians on 22 January 1941 when the advancing British tanks and Australian infantry began to enter the port.

MoD ref: CM1869

Crews of the RAAF posing on a Blenheim IV in the Middle East. They may have been part of 454 (RAAF) Squadron which was formed at Aqir in Palestine at the end of September 1942 and began training on Blenheims. After moving to Qaiyara in Iraq the following month and receiving Blenheim Vs, the squadron moved to Gianaclis in Egypt in January 1943 and began converting to Baltimores.

MoD ref: CM1821

Damaged German and Italian aircraft beside workshops near Derna in Libya, west of Tobruk. The town was first occupied by Australian troops on 30 January 1941 but then changed hands the following April when Rommel's Afrika Korps attacked.

MoD ref: CM1848

Servicing Commando and Signals Units of the RAF going ashore on the south-east tip of Sicily, soon after the assault troops of the British 8th Army landed at dawn on 10 July 1943. The Commandos helped the Royal Engineers restore the ploughed-up airfield at Pachino and the first Spitfire squadrons began to operate from there three days later. Other airfields were rapidly made serviceable.

PRO ref: DEFE 2/502

Aircraft such as these Douglas Dakotas flown out to the Mediterranean were often routed through Gibraltar, but in the early years of the war the length of the runway was inadequate. Work on extending the runway out into the sea began in 1941. An interim length of 1,550 yards was reached by April 1942 and work continued. In November 1942 the airfield played an essential role in the landings in North Africa. By January 1943 the runway was extended to its final length of 1,800 yards. Gibraltar was a main base for the invasion of southern France in August 1944.

PRO ref: AIR 27/284

Casablanca in Morocco, controlled by Vichy France, photographed on 4 April 1942. The photograph shows the Grand Jetty and a concentration of merchant ships in the centre. A 6-inch cruiser of the *Duguay-Trouin* class was directing her signal lamp towards the aircraft, and the photo-interpreters could also identify three *Alcyon* or *Simoun* destroyers on her port and starboard. The source of the photograph was not recorded in the intelligence report, but it was possibly taken by an RAF aircraft operating from Gibraltar.

PRO ref: AIR 34/743

The squadrons of No. 3 (SAAF) Bomber Wing, equipped with Martin Marauder medium bombers, found that their aircraft were often bogged down in the mud at Iesi in Italy. This type of aircraft was employed exclusively in the Mediterranean theatre, by the RAF, the RAF and the USAAF.

PRO ref: AIR 26/16

In November 1944 No. 3 (SAAF) Bomber Wing moved from Pescara on the Adriatic coast to Iesi landing ground, south-west of Ancona, as the Allied forces fought their way up the Italian peninsula through the German defences of the 'Gothic Line'. The Wing was part of the Desert Air Force, which in turn was part of the Mediterranean Tactical Air Force. Tents were set up at this base during a cold and wet winter. At least eight different types of aircraft can be seen in this photograph.

PRO ref: AIR 26/16

The remains of an Arado Ar234B photo-reconnaissance jet aircraft, radio code T9+DH, works number 140142, of *Kommando Sommer*, shot down on 12 October 1944 by P-51 Mustangs of the US 52nd Fighter Group. It fell about 10 miles north-west of Alfonsine near Lake Comacchio in Italy. The pilot, *Oberleutnant* Günther Gniesmer, was killed. The square opening on the underside of the fuselage was a camera aperture.

PRO ref: AIR 23/3460

FIGHTERS ON THE OFFENSIVE

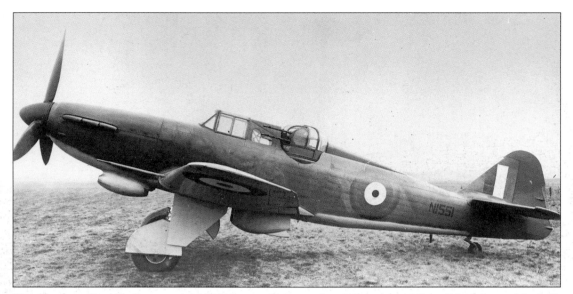

This Boulton Paul Defiant, serial N1551, was the second to be converted from Mark I to a Mark II, with the original Rolls-Royce Merlin III of 1,030 hp replaced by a Merlin XX engine of 1,260 hp. Deliveries of the Mark II to squadrons began in February 1941. Many of the aircraft were employed as nightfighters, eventually being fitted with radar. The gunner in the power-operated turret fired upwards into the belly of German bombers. This upward-firing technique was later used by German nightfighters with considerable success against RAF bombers.

PRO ref: SUPP 9/1

The Spitfire VI, fitted with a pressurized cabin, extended wingtips, a Rolls-Royce Merlin 47 engine and a four-bladed propeller, was designed to perform better at high altitude than its predecessor, the Spitfire V. This aircraft, serial BR289, was taken off the production line and tested in May 1942 by the Air Fighting Development Unit at Duxford in Cambridgeshire to assess the merits of the pressurized cabin, with favourable results.

PRO ref: AIR 2/2825

(*Opposite*) At 21.35 hours on 22 October 1941 Junkers Ju88A-4 radio code 7T+CH of *1.Küstenfliegergruppe 606* was shot down near Woore in Shropshire by Boulton Paul Defiant I, serial T3995, of 256 Squadron flown by Flight Lieutenant George B.S. Coleman with Flight Sergeant Smith in the turret. The Junkers was taking part in a bombing raid on Merseyside Docks, while the Defiant was based at Squires Gate in Lancashire. Two of the German crew, *Gefreiter* K. Hennemann and *Unteroffizier* J. Kolar, baled out and were taken prisoner. The other two, *Oberfeldwebel* Herbert Datzert, aged 26, and *Feldwebel* Erich Neukirchen, aged 24, were killed. They were buried with full military honours the following day at Stoke-on-Tern cemetery by a party from No. 5 Flying Training School at RAF Ternhill in Shropshire. The commanding officer of the RAF station also attended the funeral.

PRO ref: AIR 29/557

This Miles Master I, serial N7447, was converted to a Master II with a Bristol Mercury XX engine of 870 hp. A total of 3,450 Masters were built, both before and during the war, as two-seat advanced trainers for fighter pilots.

PRO ref: SUPP 9/1

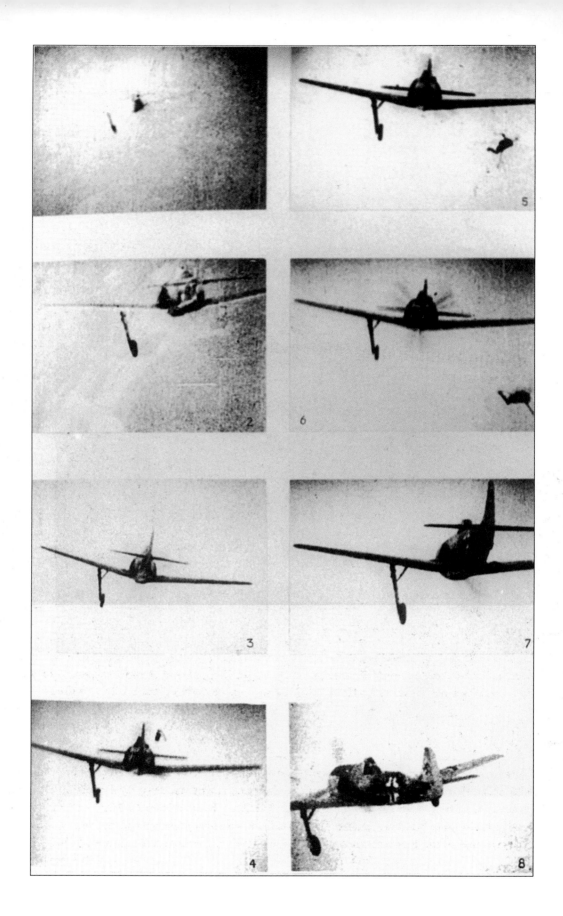

This undated photograph of a Heinkel He111 under attack accompanies a record of the so-called 'Baedecker raids' which began on 24 April 1942 against lightly defended cathedral cities in England. These day and night raids were mounted by the Luftwaffe in retaliation for attacks by Bomber Command against German cities. However, it is possible that the photograph may date from an earlier period since the He111 was too slow for daylight operations by this time.

PRO ref: AIR 41/49

(*Opposite*) This series of photographs was taken from the camera gun film of a Spitfire V in combat with a Focke-Wulf Fw190. The precise date does not appear in the records but the photographs illustrate a history of the RAF's sweeps over Northern France from 24 March to 31 May 1942, when Fighter and Bomber Commands carried out short-range attacks in daylight, partly to help ease pressure on the Russians when the Wehrmacht was attacking on the Eastern Front.

PRO ref: AIR 41/49

Men of the RAF Regiment taking over guard duties at Buckingham Palace from the Coldstream Guards. This regiment was formed on 1 February 1942, its origins stemming from the RAF's armoured car companies which from early 1922 were responsible for internal security in countries of the Middle East governed by Britain. Known as 'The Rock Apes', the men were responsible primarily for the defence of RAF airfields against air attacks, but their duties were soon expanded into other fields.

MoD ref: CH9006

(*Opposite*) This Focke-Wulf Fw190A-3, works number 313, was photographed at RAF Pembrey in Carmarthenshire after it landed there in error on 23 June 1942. It was flown by *Oberleutnant* Arnim Faber, the *Gruppen-Adjutant* of *III. Gruppe*, and was on the strength of *7./Jadgeschwader 2* based at Morlaix in Brittany. Faber was engaged in air battle with Spitfires of the Exeter and Portreath Wings, but then flew in a reciprocal direction after shooting down one of these fighters. He evidently mistook the Bristol Channel for the English Channel and then performed victory rolls over Pembrey, which was an air gunners' school, under the impression that it was Morlaix. He lowered his undercarriage while in the inverted position, rolled back and landed off a steep turn. The machine bore his single chevron insignia in front of the cross, with the vertical bar of *III. Gruppe* behind it.

PRO ref: AIR 41/49

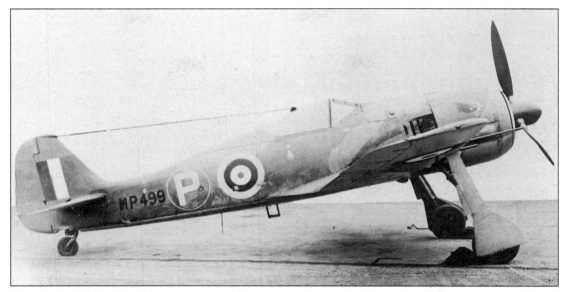

The Focke-Wulf Fw190A-3 was gratefully received by the British, who had even contemplated mounting a commando raid on an airfield in the Cherbourg peninsula to capture one of these new machines and fly it back to England. It was transported to the Royal Aircraft Establishment at Farnborough where it was given the serial number MP499 and the letter P (for prototype) before being tested in flight on 3 July 1942. After ten days, it was transferred to the Air Fighting Development Unit at Duxford, where it was tested in mock combat with RAF fighters.

PRO ref: AVIA 6/10120

The British and Canadian landings at Dieppe on 19 August 1942 were intended to bring the Luftwaffe to battle as well as to prepare for the eventual Allied invasion and the liberation of France. Fifty-six squadrons of Fighter Command took part, the aircraft including the Hawker Typhoon, which had come into service during the previous January. This machine did not prove fully satisfactory at higher altitudes but later achieved fame as a rocket-firing fighter-bomber.

PRO ref: AIR 41/49

This prototype of the Westland Welkin, serial DG558, first flew on 1 November 1942. It was developed as a twin-engined fighter for employment at high altitude but, although sixty-seven were built, it did not enter squadron service.

PRO ref: SUPP 9/1

A popular trade for WAAF volunteers was that of 'M.T. driver', which came within Group 5. Another trade, within Group 2, was 'M.T. mechanic'. This photograph was taken on 23 January 1943.

MoD ref: CH8325

The RAF's North American Mustang III, fitted with a Packard Merlin engine of 1,680 hp manufactured in America under licence with Rolls-Royce, proved to be one of the most successful fighters of the Second World War. The aircraft in this photograph was on the strength of 19 Squadron, which was first equipped with Mustang IIIs in February 1944. As part of the 2nd Tactical Air Force, 19 Squadron was engaged on fighter-bomber attacks against targets in northern France.

PRO ref: AIR 41/49

This Dornier Do217M was one of four aircraft which crashed on land during a raid on London during the night of 23/24 February 1944. It was hit by anti-aircraft fire at 10,000 feet over the north-west suburbs, causing minor damage to the fuselage, starboard engine nacelle and starboard mainplane. The crew baled out and were captured in the district of Wembley, but the aircraft flew on serenely and made a good landing on some allotments at Milton Road in Cambridge. This was the second time that a Do217 had made a good landing in England without its crew, and the RAF report paid tribute to Dr Claude Dornier on the excellence of his design. The markings on this machine were U5+DK, which identified it as *2 Staffel, 1 Gruppe, Kampfgeschwader 2 (2./KG2)*, 'D' being the aircraft's individual letter and 'K' the *2 Staffel*. White spinner tips and two white bands around the tail indicated *1 Gruppe*. The works number on the fin was 56051 and the same number appeared on the radio card as well as the nose section. However, the compass card gave the works number 6051, causing the RAF inspection team to wonder if the aircraft had been damaged and then repaired by adding part of a second aircraft. The upper surfaces were blue with mottled green while the undersurfaces were white. There was a very rough surface to the paint.

PRO ref: AIR 40/45

A V1 (V=Vergeltungswaffe) flying bomb over the English countryside on 4 July 1944. The warhead contained about 1,870 lb of high explosive. The bomb flew at a maximum speed of about 310 mph and its range was about 150 miles.

PRO ref: AIR 25/792

The V1 (top right) being pursued by a Hawker Tempest V, one of the RAF's fighters capable of catching the bomb and destroying it with cannon fire. These photographs were taken by Lieutenant Schumacher flying at an altitude of 2,000 feet in a Lockheed F-5 of the USAAF, a photo-reconnaissance version of the P-38 twin-boom fighter.

PRO ref: AIR 25/792

The first V1 flying bombs were launched against the London area in the early morning of 13 June 1944 and the last fell on 29 March 1945. They were inaccurate and normally fell on civilian targets. Nearly 4,000 bombs were brought down by aircraft, anti-aircraft fire or balloon cables. However, V1s killed 6,139 people and seriously injured 17,239 others. This example of their work was photographed at Harwood Terrace in Fulham, where two-storey terraced houses together with the Anderson air raid shelters in their gardens were demolished or damaged.

PRO ref: HO 192/73

The wreckage of a French train carrying V1 flying bombs, photographed after an attack by RAF's fighter-bombers of the 2nd Tactical Air Force on 1 September 1944.

PRO ref: AIR 41/49

A captured German photograph showing a V1 flying bomb on a trailer. The German designation of the V1 was Fieseler Fi 103.

PRO ref: AIR 40/2532

A V2 long-range rocket, for which the German designation was A4. This was one of a trainload captured by the US First Army at Bromskirchen railway station, near Kassel in Germany. The warhead was lying in front of the main body of the rocket. The first V2 exploded in Chiswick on 8 September 1944 and the last, the 1,115th, at Orpington on 27 March 1945. Like the V1 flying bombs, V2 rockets were inaccurate and intended to spread terror among civilians. They killed 2,855 people and seriously injured 6,268 others. There was no method of shooting them down and the only defence was to bomb the launching sites and supply depots.

PRO ref: CAB 98/62

(*Opposite*) An official photograph taken in August 1944 of Wing Commander J.E. 'Johnny' Johnson, the fighter pilot who was credited with the destruction of thirty-five enemy aircraft and awarded the DSO and two bars, the DFC and bar and the American DFC. He is shown being greeted by his labrador Sally on return from a sortie, with his Spitfire in the background. At the time, he commanded an RCAF Spitfire Wing in Normandy, part of the 2nd Tactical Air Force.

PRO ref: INF 2/43

This Spitfire XIV, serial RM784, fitted with a balloon rear-view hood and a cut-down rear fuselage, was subjected to spinning trials by the Aircraft and Armament Experimental Establishment at Boscombe Down in Wiltshire during March 1945. The only effect of the modifications appeared to be a slight increase in the number of turns required to recover.

PRO ref: AVIA 18/682

This Hawker Typhoon IB, serial MN861, was tested during September 1944 at the Aircraft and Armament Experimental Establishment at Boscombe Down in Wiltshire. It carried double-tiered rocket projectiles, making sixteen in all. The rockets in this photograph were fitted with 60 lb semi-armour piercing warheads, normally referred to as high explosive. They were used mainly against enemy armoured columns and ground positions.

PRO ref: AVIA 18/1049

THE ANTI-SHIPPING
WAR

On 12 August 1944 twelve Beaufighter TFXs of 236 Squadron and twelve more of 404 (RCAF) Squadron, operating from Davidstow Moor in Cornwall, attacked the heavily armed German *Sperrbrecher 7* (formerly the *Sauerland* of 7,087 tons) off Royan in the mouth of the Gironde. The vessel, which was employed as a flak-ship and for exploding mines, was badly damaged by rocket projectiles and machine-gun fire. She was finished off by the cruiser HMS *Diadem* and two destroyers, which sped to the locality. One Beaufighter was shot down but the crew was picked up from their dinghy by a destroyer.

PRO ref: AIR 15/472

This prototype of the Short Sunderland III, serial T9042, made its first flight on 28 June 1941. It was fitted with antennae for air to surface vessel (ASV) Mark II radar and a new type of planing surface on the bottom of the hull. This variant began to replace earlier Sunderlands in December 1941.

PRO ref: SUPP 9/1

At 18.40 hours on 27 November 1940 an oil bomb dropped during an air raid on RAF Mount Batten, a flying boat station near Plymouth in Devon, scored a direct hit on a hangar and destroyed it. Other bombs set oil tanks on fire at Turnchapel, a quarter of a mile away. The tanks burned for ninety hours before they were extinguished, illuminating the surrounding district and providing an excellent marker for other German bombers.

PRO ref: AIR 27/149

Within the hangar, Sunderland I serial N9048 of 10 (RAAF) Squadron, which had been beached during the afternoon, caught fire and was destroyed. At 20.15 hours on the same evening, a bomb from a further air attack hit Sunderland I serial P9601 from the same squadron, when it was at moorings in the Cattewater. This flying boat also caught fire and sank with its load of depth charges and anti-submarine bombs.

PRO ref: AIR 27/149

A steel mat was laid at Rhu, near Helensburgh and a Saro Lerwick flying boat, serial L7248, was successfully beached. This was the prototype Lerwick, with twin fins and rudders; later machines had only a single fin and rudder. The Lerwick proved an unstable machine, with several technical faults. Only twenty-one were built, first entering service in December 1939. After several losses, the remainder were withdrawn in October 1942.

PRO ref: AVIA 19/484

On 25 September 1940 a Sunderland of 10 (RAAF) Squadron, flown by Squadron Leader W.H. Garing, based at Mount Batten in Devon but detached to Oban in Argyllshire, came across this lifeboat far out in the North Atlantic when returning from a patrol over an inward-bound convoy. The lifeboat was heading towards Britain and children could be seen on board. Garing attempted to alight but the sea was too rough. The crew made contact with a Sunderland of 210 Squadron from Oban, flown by Flight Lieutenant E.F. Baker, which had relieved them over the convoy, and guided it towards the lifeboat. The crew of the first Sunderland dropped a lifejacket with a message telling the occupants of the lifeboat that help was on its way. Shortage of fuel then compelled them to return to Oban.

PRO ref: AIR 27/149

The second Sunderland arrived over the lifeboat and dropped food for the occupants. It then returned to the convoy and informed the Senior Naval Officer on the destroyer HMS *Anthony*. The Sunderland guided this destroyer to the lifeboat and the survivors were picked up three hours after they were spotted. They turned out to be forty adults and six children in lifeboat no. 12 from *City of Benares*, a lightly armed passenger liner of 11,081 tons which had been torpedoed and sunk by the Type VIIIB U-boat *U-48* eight days previously, while en route from Liverpool to Quebec and Montreal. This vessel was carrying passengers who included many children being evacuated to sponsored homes in North America, as well as adult refugees from Europe. Only 150 of the adult passengers and crew on the vessel survived, and only 13 of the 100 children. Many drowned when lifeboats capsized or overturned while being lowered into tempestuous seas, and others died of immersion hypothermia in waterlogged lifeboats or when clinging to liferafts. Most of the survivors were picked up by the destroyer HMS *Hurricane* the day after the liner was sunk. The survivors rescued from lifeboat no. 12, who had been assumed dead by the authorities, were suffering from severe exposure. HMS *Anthony* left the convoy to take them to Gourock. *U-48* was sunk in October 1943 after a war career in which she sank fifty-nine vessels.

PRO ref: AIR 27/149

This German *Sperrbrecher* was photographed in the North Sea on 18 April 1941. She was one of several large merchant vessels employed for destroying mines and as escort vessels heavily armed with flak guns. The hulls of these ships were reinforced with concrete for protection against magnetic mines sitting on the bottom of the sea. The origin of this photograph was not recorded in the RAF intelligence document.

PRO ref: AIR 34/743

At 08.01 hours on 23 July 1941 Lockheed Hudson V serial AM536 of 233 Squadron from Aldergrove in County Antrim, flown by Pilot Officer Down, was escorting westbound Convoy OG–69 in position 5400N 1355W when a Focke-Wulf Condor approached at low level. Down dived towards it at full speed, opened fire with his front guns and closed to 100 feet. His gunners then fired from point-blank range, when below and on the port side of their target. The port engine of the Condor was set on fire and the aircraft dived into the sea. The six men in the German crew were picked up from their dinghy by a British corvette, with one man suffering from burns. This photograph was taken from the Hudson with an F24 camera at 08.11 hours.

PRO ref: AIR 27/1438

This interesting photograph shows how well the camouflage of Lockheed Hudson III serial T9444 of 206 Squadron blended into the countryside of Northern Ireland. The squadron was based at Aldergrove from August 1941 to July 1942, engaged on hunting U-boats in the Atlantic and the approaches to Liverpool and the Clyde.

PRO ref: AIR 15/470

On 15 September 1941 six Blenheim IVs of 114 Squadron from West Raynham in Norfolk attacked an eastbound convoy of seven merchant vessels, escorted by four flak-ships and a larger warship, when 15 miles north-east of Borkum. The crews reported hits on two merchant vessels, one of which was hit on the starboard bow by two 500 lb bombs and incendiaries. The German freighter *Johann Wessels* of 4,601 tons was sunk in this attack. The Blenheims were attacked by two Messerschmitt Bf109s and some were damaged, although all returned safely. This photograph was taken with an F24 camera mounted vertically in the fuselage, with a mirror facing aft.

PRO ref: AIR 14/3670

On 17 June 1942 the escort destroyer HMS *Wild Swan* of 1,150 tons displacement was damaged by a German air attack about 100 miles south of Bantry Bay in Eire. She then sank after a collision with a Spanish fishing vessel. At 03.00 hours the following day, Sunderland III of 10 (RAAF) Squadron, with Flight Lieutenant Maurice L. Judell as captain, set off from Mount Batten in Devon to search for survivors. At 10.05 hours the aircraft exchanged signals with the destroyer HMS *Vansittart* and continued the search. A large oil patch was spotted twenty-five minutes later, then two dinghies and four liferafts (as shown here), and then a motor boat.

PRO ref: AIR 27/151

The destroyer HMS *Vansittart* was guided to the area, escorted by two Beaufighters, and picked up the survivors. Unfortunately Judell and his crew were killed only four days later, on 21 June 1942. They were in Sunderland III serial W3999, in company with a Whitley of 58 Squadron from St Eval in Cornwall, in a hunt for a dinghy containing four members of a Wellington VIII of 172 Squadron from Chivenor in Devon, which had come down in the Bay of Biscay. Both the Sunderland and the Whitley were attacked by an Arado Ar196 seaplane. The inner starboard engine of the Sunderland was hit and it alighted on the sea. Then the petrol tanks appeared to explode and the seaplane disappeared, with no trace of survivors.

PRO ref: AIR 27/151

Four views of an airborne lifeboat being carried by a Lockheed Hudson, then released, then descending by parachutes, and then with the sails being set. The lifeboat was also fitted with an engine which gave a range of about 80 miles. It carried food, water, a wireless and survival equipment. These photographs of a practice exercise were taken in early 1943.

PRO ref: AIR 15/470

The air/sea rescue Lysanders worked in concert with the RAF's high-speed launches. Although this photograph was taken for publicity purposes, many genuine rescues did take place and the existence of this service around the coasts of Britain provided a boost to the morale of operational airmen.

PRO ref: INF 2/45

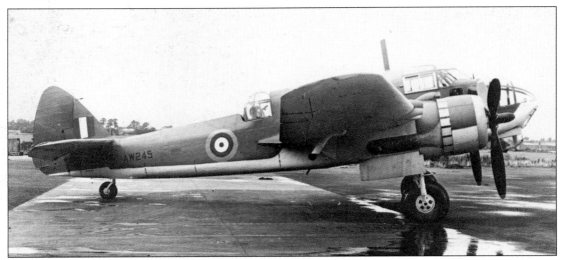

The Bristol Beaufort II torpedo bomber, fitted with twin Wasp engines of 1,200 hp, was introduced into squadron service at the end of October 1941. It was an improvement on the Beaufort I since it was easier to fly on one engine. This example, serial AW245, was the second to be built.

PRO ref: SUPP 9/1

This Bristol Beaufort II, serial AW304, was part of the Torpedo Development Unit at Gosport in Hampshire, where it was fitted with dive-brakes and tested during August 1942. Mark XII torpedoes were dropped during the trials and the results were considered satisfactory, apart from suggestions for improving the pilot's controls of the dive-brakes. Some 300 production Beaufort IAs, together with a few earlier aircraft, were fitted with the dive-brakes but they proved unpopular with pilots because of asymmetrical opening and were later locked closed.

PRO ref: AVIA 16/72

This Lancaster III, serial JA893, of 106 Squadron based at Syerston in Nottinghamshire, ditched in the North Sea about 200 miles from the English coast at about 05.00 hours on 4 September 1943, when returning from a raid on Berlin. Flown by Squadron Leader David W.S. Howroyd, the aircraft had been badly damaged by a Messerschmitt Bf110 nightfighter, with the bomb aimer killed and both the rear gunner and flight engineer wounded, although fire from the mid-upper turret had destroyed the German aircraft. Howroyd made a good ditching and the six surviving members got into their circular H-type dinghy. The wireless operator had been in touch with base and the homing pigeon carried in the aircraft was released. The Lancaster remained afloat and they stayed attached to it by means of the dinghy rope, but meanwhile the rear gunner died.

PRO ref: AIR 27/836

(*Opposite*) Two high-speed launches of the Royal Navy were guided by radio to the lifeboat by the Hudson flown by Flight Sergeant E. Palmer. The launches reached the lifeboat at 16.00 hours and the Lancaster men were taken on board. The flight engineer's wounds were attended to, and the launches set off for Immingham, near Grimsby, where they docked at 05.45 hours the next day after a rough passage. Following a short leave the four uninjured men rejoined 106 Squadron and crewed up with three other men. They took off in Lancaster III serial DV273 on 8 October 1943 for a raid on Hannover but the aircraft failed to return. The only survivor was the new Canadian bomb aimer, Pilot Officer L.D. Cromb, who became a PoW.

PRO ref: AIR 27/836

At 06.40 hours on 4 September 1943 two air/sea rescue Hudsons of 279 Squadron, flown by Flying Officer J. Tait and Pilot Officer J.E. Watts, took off from Bircham Newton in Norfolk to search for the downed Lancaster in response to the distress calls. They found the aircraft and the dinghy at 08.57 hours and Tait dropped a Lindholme dinghy. This was a large dinghy in the centre of four containers connected to each other by a length of rope with Kapok floats, but the dinghy did not open and one container burst. The ditched crew hauled in the other containers, which contained rations. Another Hudson flown by Warrant Officer J. Passlow took off at 09.53 hours, carrying an airborne lifeboat, led by a fourth Hudson flown by Flight Sergeant E. Palmer. Watts left the crashed Lancaster, met these two aircraft and guided them to the crash site, which they reached at 10.31 hours. The lifeboat was dropped successfully and the five Lancaster men got into it. They started the motor and set off towards the English coast, towing the dinghy with the body of the rear gunner. Palmer continued to circle above them, while the other three Hudsons returned to Bircham Newton.

PRO ref: AIR 27/836

This Spitfire VB, serial W3760, was converted to a floatplane and tested at the Marine Experimental Establishment at Helensburgh in Dunbarton during March 1943. The fin area was increased and a four-bladed propeller was fitted. However, the version finally chosen for the Fleet Air Arm was the carrier-borne Seafire IB, with a retractable deck arrester hook under the rear fuselage.

PRO ref: AVIA 19/606

In June 1944 the Lockheed Ventura Vs of 22 (SAAF) Squadron were moved from Durban to Gibraltar, to carry out anti-submarine patrols in the western Mediterranean. The Ventura, a military version of the civil Lodestar, was originally employed by the RAF as a light bomber but soon transferred to maritime duties. The aircraft letter F of this Ventura, serial 6469, was used as the centre of its Afrikaans nickname 'Ou Flerrie' (meaning 'Old Flirt') painted on the fuselage.

PRO ref: AIR 27/285

Part of an attack made on 1 June 1944 by a force of twenty-four Beaufighter TFXs from Egypt against a large enemy convoy attempting to relieve a German garrison in Crete. The Beaufighters were from 252 Squadron at Mersa Matruh, 227 Squadron and 16 (SAAF) Squadron at Berka III, and 603 Squadron at Gambut. Flying Officer George G. Tuffin, a Canadian in 252 Squadron, had just fired his rockets against this German armed trawler and submarine hunter *UJ2105* of 350 tons. The vessel burned out and sank.

PRO ref: AIR 27/1509

The German armed merchant vessel *Gertrud* of 1,960 tons, part of the convoy trying to relieve the German garrison in Crete, under rocket attack on 1 June 1944 by a Beaufighter TFX of 252 Squadron flown by Flying Officer William Davenport. The vessel was badly damaged but was towed into Heraklion, where she blew up the following night after being hit by bombs dropped by Baltimores of 15 (SAAF) Squadron from Landing Ground 91 in Egypt. Davenport was shot down and taken prisoner on 19 June 1944.

PRO ref: AIR 27/1509

On 8 July 1944 Sunderland III serial W4030 of 10 (RAAF) Squadron based at Mount Batten in Devon, flown by Flying Officer W.S. Tilley, attacked the Type VIIC *U-243* off the Brest peninsula. Both the U-boat and the Sunderland opened fire. Six 250 lb depth charges were then dropped, straddling the U-boat, which was destroyed. The German crew launched dinghies and the Sunderland crew chivalrously dropped another dinghy to survivors swimming in the water.

PRO ref: AIR 37/1231

On 11 June 1944 Canso A serial 9842 (a Canadian-built version of the Consolidated Catalina) flown by Flying Officer L. Sherman of 162 Squadron and based at Reykjavik in Iceland, encountered the Type VIIC U-boat *U-980* off the Shetlands. Both opened fire and then the Canso straddled its target with four 250 lb depth charges. The U-boat sank, leaving an oil patch and about thirty-five survivors in the water.

PRO ref: AIR 37/1231

This Beaufighter TFX, serial NT921, was tested by the Aircraft and Armament Establishment at Boscombe Down in Wiltshire in late June 1944, after modification to carry two 500 lb general-purpose bombs under the fuselage and two more of 250 lb under the wings. This mark of Beaufighter was employed by Coastal Command or anti-shipping squadrons abroad on attacks against enemy vessels. The normal armament consisted of machine-guns and either a torpedo or rockets.

PRO ref: AVIA 18/1576

(*Opposite, top*) An attack on 24 August 1944 by ten Beaufighter TFXs of 236 Squadron and ten of 404 (RCAF) Squadron, from Coastal Command's Davidstow Strike Wing in Cornwall, against the German torpedo boat *T24* of 1,294 tons (foreground) and the 'Narvik' class destroyer *Z24* of 2,603 tons (background) off Le Verdon in the Gironde estuary. Both warships were sunk by rocket hits above and below the waterline. Fifteen Beaufighters were hit by return fire but all returned to Davidstow Moor or landed at Vannes in France.

PRO ref: AIR 37/1231

The German armed merchant vessel *Carola* of 1,348 tons under attack south-east of Athens on 6 September 1944 by eight Beaufighter TFXs of 252 Squadron and four of 603 Squadron, from Gambut in Egypt. The formation was led by Wing Commander Denis O. Butler, who fired the rockets shown splashing in this photograph. The vessel was badly damaged but reached Piraeus, where she went into dry dock. She was sunk later by the Germans as a blockship in the port.

PRO ref: AIR 27/1509

Incorrectly dated 25 May 1944 in the PRO reference, this photograph was in fact taken on 25 August 1944. On that day, forty-four Beaufighter TFXs from four squadrons attacked a German convoy off Schiermonnikoog in the Dutch Frisian Islands. The four were 144 Squadron from Strubby in Lincolnshire, 254 Squadron from North Coates in Lincolnshire, together with 455 (RAAF) and 489 (RNZAF) Squadrons from Langham in Norfolk. The convoy consisted of six or eight armed merchant ships with ten escorts. The Beaufighters attacked with torpedoes, rocket projectiles and cannon fire. All torpedoes missed but the German minesweeper *M347* of 637 tons was sunk. No aircraft were lost.

PRO ref: AIR 37/1231/80

(*Opposite*) On 24 October, five Beaufighter TFXs of 252 Squadron from Gambut attacked the German headquarters in the Greek Island of Kalymnos. The rockets shown in this photograph were fired by Warrant Officer W.K. Ashley. The building was left on fire and the garrison surrendered shortly afterwards.

PRO ref: AIR 27/1509

The German minelayer and troop transport *Drache* of 1,870 tons under attack at Port Vathi in Samos on 22 September 1944 by eight Beaufighter TFXs of 252 Squadron and four of 603 Squadron, from Gambut in Egypt. The formation was led by Wing Commander Denis O. Butler.

PRO ref: AIR 27/1509

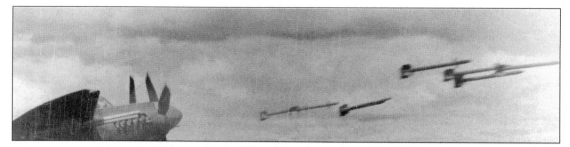

The Banff Strike Wing of Coastal Command was formed in September 1944 to join in attacks against German-controlled shipping along the coasts of Norway. These ships carried essential war materials such as Swedish iron ore from Narvik to Rotterdam. The aircraft in the Wing were de Havilland Mosquito VIs and Bristol Beaufighter TFXs. Most of these were armed with four 20 mm cannons, four .303 inch machine-guns and eight rocket projectiles. The rockets in this photograph were fired from a Mosquito. Each carried 25 lb solid shot warheads, designed to penetrate the hull of a vessel below the waterline.

PRO ref: AIR 26/597

A close-up of the *Lynx* of 1,367 tons, under cannon and machine-gun fire while eight rockets were streaking towards her. She was sunk, as well as the troopship *Tyrifjord* of 3,080 tons, but one Beaufighter was shot down.

PRO ref: AIR 26/597

An attack on 21 October 1944 by Beaufighters of 404 (RCAF) Squadron and Mosquitos of 235 and 248 Squadrons of the Banff Strike Wing, led by a Belgian serving in the RAF, Wing Commander J.M. Maurice (whose real name was Max Guedj), against shipping in Haugesund. Two vessels were sunk: *Eckenheim* of 1,923 tons and *Vestra* of 1,432 tons, while one Mosquito was shot down.

PRO ref: AIR 26/597

Within the Banff Strike Wing, Mosquito VIs in a special detachment of 248 Squadron had been modified so that the four 20 mm cannons in the nose were replaced with a Molins anti-tank gun of 57 mm calibre, firing 6 lb shells at a rate of about two shells per minute from a magazine of twenty-five rounds. These were known as Mosquito XVIIIs or 'Tsetses' and they scored several successes. One of these was on 12 December 1944 when twenty-three Mosquitos of 143, 235, 248 and 333 Squadrons attacked a convoy off Eid Fjord. This remarkable photograph shows a shell streaking towards a vessel on that day with two Mosquitos just visible above the mast-tops. The *Wartheland* of 3,678 tons was sunk and the *Molla* of 815 tons was badly damaged in this attack.

PRO ref: AIR 26/597

An attack on 23 March 1945 off Aalesund by Mosquitos of 143 Squadron, part of the Banff Strike Wing, led by Wing Commander Christopher Foxley-Norris. The *Lysaker* of 910 tons was sunk, but two Mosquitos were shot down.

PRO ref: AIR 26/597

REAPING THE WHIRLWIND

An undated publicity photograph showing the last stages in an assembly line of Handley Page Halifax IIs. Production Halifax Is first entered squadron service in November 1940 and the Halifax II followed in September 1941. Variants of this four-engined bomber continued with the RAF until March 1952.

PRO ref: INF 2/45

On 7 April 1941 eight Blenheim IVs of Bomber Command's 139 Squadron, based at Horsham St Faith in Norfolk, made a daylight attack on iron and steel works at Ijmuiden in the Netherlands. On this photograph the photo-interpreters circled two 500 lb bombs falling towards a large building, probably a power plant. Damage was caused to the target but one Blenheim was lost.

PRO ref: AIR 14/3668

(*Opposite*) The prototype of the Avro Lancaster, serial BT308, was known as the Manchester III when it made its maiden flight on 9 January 1941. It was a converted Manchester airframe fitted with four Rolls-Royce Merlin engines instead of two Rolls-Royce Vultures. Ventral and dorsal turrets were not fitted on this prototype and it retained the triple fins of the Manchester I instead of the twin fins of production Lancasters. It was developed into the most famous heavy bomber to enter service in the RAF during the Second World War.

PRO ref: SUPP 9/1

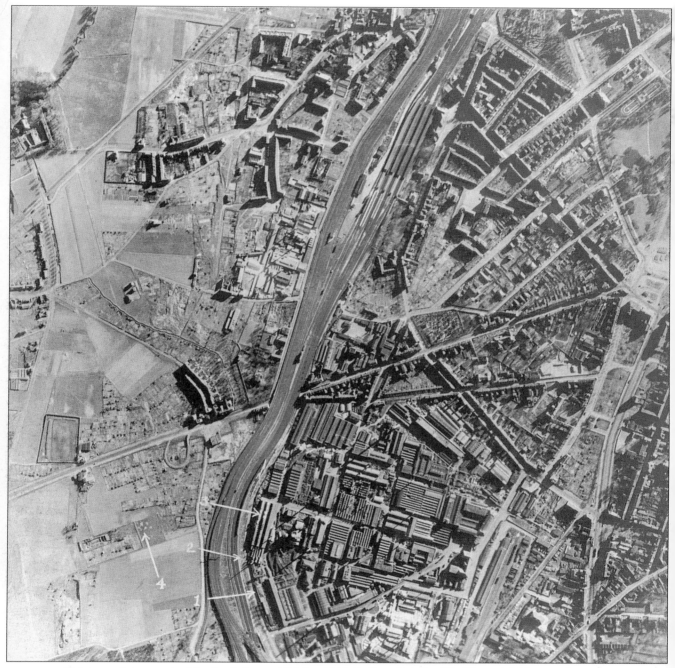

Cologne photographed in daylight on 12 March 1941 from Spitfire PR ID, serial X4712, flown by Flight Lieutenant N.H. Messervey of No. 3 Photographic Reconnaissance Unit based at Oakington in Cambridgeshire. The city had been bombed on the night of 10/11 March 1941, as well as on several occasions during the previous weeks, but the first 'thousand bomber' raid was not mounted against Cologne until 30/31 May 1942.

PRO ref: AIR 29/432

This clear photograph of the sports stadium in Berlin, where the Olympic Games were held in August 1936, was probably an enlargement of the original exposure. A series of photographs of Berlin was taken during daylight on 14 March 1941 by Squadron Leader P.B.B. Ogilvie in a Spitfire PR ID of No. 3 Photographic Unit based at Oakington in Cambridgeshire, a unit which came under the control of Bomber Command from November 1940 to June 1941.

PRO ref: AIR 14/3668

Oil tanks in Rotterdam photographed in daylight on 19 March 1941 by a Spitfire PR ID of No. 3 Photographic Reconnaissance Unit based at Oakington in Cambridgeshire, after a series of small attacks by aircraft of Bomber Command. The photo-interpreters annotated the photograph:

1. One large tank of 150 ft diameter destroyed by fire.
2. A group of ten small and five medium tanks completely destroyed.
3. A direct hit on a 150 ft diameter tank.
4. Small building damaged at north-west end.
5. Hit on road between twelve small tanks.
6. Crater between twelve small tanks.

7. Crater (near miss) to 150 ft diameter tank.

8. Crater on embankment 60 ft from tank.

9. Crater in open ground.

10. Small crater 50 ft from tank.

11. Slight discoloration of roof of building.

12. Roof of four-bay building and part of building darkened, possibly by fire.

13. Blast walls and camouflage on buildings.

PRO ref: AIR 14/3668

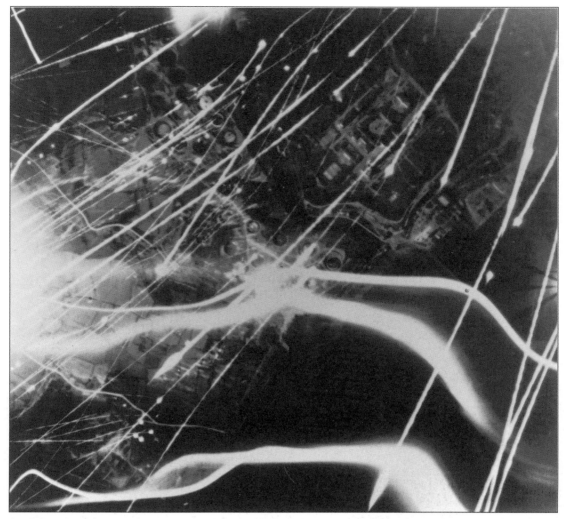

A night photograph of the port of Brest in France, taken at 03.20 hours on 15 April 1941 by a Wellington IC of 99 Squadron based at Waterbeach in Cambridgeshire, during an attack against the German battleships *Scharnhorst* and *Gneisenau* and the cruiser *Admiral Hipper*. It shows the effect of searchlights and tracer fire during the period of exposure of the negative in an F24 camera mounted vertically in the aircraft's fuselage.

PRO ref: AIR 14/3668

This photograph of Berlin was taken on the night of 9/10 April 1941 with the aid of a photo-flash dropped from 11,000 feet by a Hampden of 49 Squadron based at Scampton in Lincolnshire. The 4.5 inch photo-flash could either be dropped through the flare chute or released from a bomb rack. It was detonated in mid-air by a time-burning fuse which usually exploded at two-thirds of the altitude of the aircraft, giving a duration of light of one-tenth of a second. This is the suburb of Siemenstadt, to the north-west of Berlin, with the River Spree at the bottom of the photograph, which was marred only by searchlight tracks.

PRO ref: AIR 14/3668

On 27 December 1941 thirteen Blenheim IVs of 114 Squadron from West Raynham in Norfolk raided the German fighter base at Herdla, near Bergen, as part of a diversion when British commandos landed at Vaasgö. The aircraft attacked at low level, dropping 250 lb general-purpose bombs and 25 lb incendiaries, while firing from rear turrets at ground installations. They were met with inaccurate heavy flak and some light flak. No Blenheims were lost but two collided and crashed. Some remains of these aircraft can still be seen in the water.

PRO ref: AIR 34/745

(*Opposite*) The devastation in the centre of Rotterdam caused by Junkers Ju87 dive bombers during their attack of 14 May 1940, photographed by a Blenheim IV of Bomber Command on 16 July 1941. A new railway station and theatre had been built on a cleared site where 20,000 buildings had been destroyed by the Luftwaffe.

PRO ref: AIR 14/3669

This photograph of the chalk cliffs of Cap d'Antifer near Le Havre, taken in the autumn of 1941, led British scientists to suspect that the point arrowed was a German *Würzburg* radar installation, but more information was required.

PRO ref: AIR 20/1631

On 8 March 1942 twelve Douglas Boston IIIs of 88 and 226 Squadrons, part of Bomber Command's 2 Group, made a low-level attack on the Ford truck factory at Poissy near Paris, causing considerable damage. One Boston was lost.

PRO ref: AIR 34/745

(*Opposite*) This paraboloid reflector dish of a German *Würzburg* radar station near the village of St Bruneval near Le Havre was photographed on 5 December 1941 in a daring low-level sortie by Flight Lieutenant A.E. 'Tony' Hill, flying in Spitfire VD (known as a PR IVD) serial R7044 of No. 1 Photographic Reconnaissance Unit based at Benson in Oxfordshire. The photographs led to a raid on 27/28 February 1942 when paratroops dropped from Whitley Vs of 51 Squadron were supported by commandos landed from the sea. The raiding party was accompanied by Flight Sergeant C.W.H. Cox, an RAF radar mechanic who volunteered to select any equipment of interest. They brought back the receiver of the radar, the amplifier, the pulse generator, the transmitter, details of the operating method and German prisoners.

PRO ref: AIR 20/1631

Le Havre was attacked in daylight on 16 April 1942 by twelve Boston IIIs of 226 Squadron from Swanton Morley in Suffolk. The photograph shows bomb bursts on the railway station as well as on the Bassin de la Barre and the Bassin Vauban. All aircraft returned, although one was damaged by flak.

PRO ref: AIR 34/743

In the early afternoon of 23 July 1942 two Douglas Boston IIIs of 107 Squadron, flown by Flight Lieutenant R.J.N. McLachlan and Pilot Officer P.K. Burley, made a low-level attack with bombs and machine-guns against a chemical factory at Sluiskil, alongside a canal leading to the River Scheldt in the south-west of the Netherlands. The crews evaded Messerschmitt Bf109s on both outward and return journeys and were met by flak over land, but they returned safely to their base at Great Massingham in Norfolk. This photograph showed their spectacular results. The German weekly situation report read: 'In the ammonia factory at Sluiskil the engine room, the electric power station, the sulphuric acid section and the gas section were destroyed. For the time being production came to a 100 per cent stop.'

PRO ref: AIR 34/745

One of the early attacks made by the United States Eighth Air Force after its arrival in England took place on 2 October 1942 when eleven DB-7 Bostons bombed German E-boats and R-boats in the docks at Le Havre. The aircraft dropped forty-four 500 lb general-purpose bombs at 14.31 hours and all returned safely. This photograph captured a Boston over the target.

PRO ref: AIR 34/745

(*Opposite, top*) Bristol Blenheim and Douglas Boston squadrons of Bomber Command's 2 Group took part in the combined raid on Dieppe, being given the tasks of close support to the ground troops and laying smokescreens. This Boston III was photographed laying a smokescreen on the day of the landings, 19 August 1942. These aircraft were fitted with four L-shaped pipes protruding from the closed bomb-bay. The Douglas Boston III was first supplied to an RAF squadron in September 1941 but did not become operational until the following February.

PRO ref: AIR 41/49

(*Opposite, bottom*) Düsseldorf photographed on 12 September 1942 from Spitfire PR IV serial BR661 flown by Pilot Officer Barraclough of No. 1 Photographic Reconnaissance Unit based at Benson. Bomber Command had despatched 479 aircraft to this target two nights previously, resulting in extensive damage and heavy loss of life, for the loss of thirty-three aircraft. Photo-interpreters were able to determine from this photograph that the roof over the platforms of the main railway station had been demolished by a heavy bomb and that half the station buildings had been wrecked.

PRO ref: AIR 34/743

The RAF station at Wyton, near Huntingdon, was opened in 1937. During the Second World War it became one of the main airfields used by Bomber Command's No. 8 (Pathfinder Force) Group. This photograph was taken on 21 October 1951 and showed the three runways, one of 2,000 yards and two of 1,400 yards.

PRO ref: AIR 14/3702

(*Opposite*) Genoa was photographed on 11 November 1942 from Mosquito PR IV, serial DZ352, of 540 Squadron based at Benson, flown by Pilot Officer M.A. Mortimer. The Italian port had been bombed from England on the night of 22/23 October 1942, causing considerable damage to the dock area and lowering the morale of the Genoese. Mortimer and his navigator, Flight Sergeant M. Pike, flew on a long daylight sortie over the Alps to Savona and Genoa, returning over Toulon and finally landing at Lympne in Kent to refuel.

PRO ref: AIR 34/743

This photograph was taken at RAF Syerston in Nottinghamshire shortly before Wing Commander Guy P. Gibson of 106 Squadron was posted on 14 March 1943 to command 617 Squadron, the famous 'dam busters'. Left to right: Squadron Leader John H. Searby (Flight Commander), Wing Commander Guy Gibson (Commanding Officer), Squadron Leader Peter Ward-Hunt (Flight Commander). Searby and Ward-Hunt survived the war but Gibson was killed when flying a Mosquito of 627 Squadron from Coningsby in Lincolnshire during an attack by Bomber Command on Mönchengladbach in Germany on 19/20 September 1944. The Mosquito crashed in Holland and Wing Commander Guy Gibson VC DSO DFC was buried, together with his navigator, Squadron Leader J.B. Warwick DFC, in the Roman Catholic cemetery at Steenbergen-en-Kruisland.

PRO ref: AIR 27/839

(*Opposite, bottom*) The 'Upkeep' mine, or bouncing bomb, fitted to Wing Commander Guy Gibson's Lancaster III, letter G serial ED932. In its final cylindrical form it was 60 inches in length, 50 inches in diameter, contained 6,600 lb of explosive and was fitted with three hydrostatic pistols set to detonate 30 feet below the surface of the water.

PRO ref: AIR 14/840

The Möhne dam, photographed on 3 April 1943, before the attack on the night of 16/17 May, from Spitfire PR XI, serial BS499, flown by Flying Officer J.R. Brew of 541 Squadron based at Benson. The aircraft carried two F52 cameras fitted vertically. The focal lengths were 36 inches and each magazine contained 500 exposures of 8½ inches by 7 inches.

PRO ref: AIR 34/609

One of the modified Lancaster IIIs which took part in the dam-busting raid was serial ED825/G, which was delivered to Scampton only a few hours before it took off on 16 May 1943. The dorsal gun turret and part of the fuselage belly had been removed to make way for the 'Upkeep' mine and its spinning motor. It was flown by Flight Lieutenant J.C. McCarthy DFC, an American who had joined the RCAF before his own country entered the war and wore both Canadian and USA shoulder tabs. He and his crew attacked the Sorpe dam and returned safely.

PRO ref: AVIA 18/715

The Möhne dam photographed from Spitfire PR XI serial EN343 of 542 Squadron from Benson, flown by Flying Officer F.G. Fray, a few hours after the attack on 17 May 1943. It shows the water still pouring through the breach, which was about 230 ft wide at the crown narrowing to about 130 ft at the base. The upstream lake had been partly drained. The main power station at the base of the dam wall had disappeared but the auxiliary power station remained standing. The northern embankment had been completely destroyed while the southern embankment had been broken in several places.

PRO ref: AIR 34/609

The Sorpe dam photographed from Spitfire **PR XI** serial EN343 of 542 Squadron from Benson, flown by Flying Officer F.G. Fray, a few hours after the attack on 17 May 1943. Two mines were dropped but the dam was not breached, since it was of stronger construction than the other two dams which were attacked. Nevertheless the parapet on the upstream side of the dam wall was damaged for a length of about 200 feet and some water had run into the compensating basin. The level of the water had not changed, although the Germans reduced it later for safety reasons.

PRO ref: AIR 34/609

The Ruhr valley at Foendenburg, 13 miles downstream from the Möhne dam, photographed from Spitfire PR XI serial EN343 of 542 Squadron from Benson, flown by Flying Officer F.G. Fray, a few hours after the attack on 17 May 1943. It showed that the railway and road bridges had been completely destroyed, while the railway station and sidings were inundated and several coaches swept off the track. A power station was isolated and a small factory partly submerged.

PRO ref: AIR 34/609

This German photograph of an unidentified Lancaster washed up on a beach may be serial ED877/G, flown by Squadron Leader Henry M. Young. The aircraft was shot down on 17 May 1943 when crossing the Dutch coast north of Ijmuiden on its return journey, after dropping a mine which exploded against the wall of the Möhne dam. All seven crew members lost their lives.

PRO ref: AIR 20/4367

An undated German photograph showing the Möhne dam protected by balloons after the attack on the night of 16/17 May 1943.

PRO ref: AIR 20/4367

An undated German photograph showing water still pouring through the Eder dam after the attack on the night of 16/17 May 1943.

PRO ref: AIR 20/4367

Part of the town of Kassel, 30 miles downstream from the Eder dam, photographed on 18 May 1943 from Spitfire PR XI serial EN411, flown by Flying Officer D.G. Scott of 542 Squadron at Benson. It showed that the Fulda river was still swollen, over a month after the dam-busting raid. The low-lying district of Unter Neustadt was still swamped, affecting bridges, main roads, the river dock, a railway track and a power station.

PRO ref: AIR 34/609

Before the attack

After the attack

The existence of the German rocket establishment on the island of Peenemünde off the Baltic coast, where research and manufacture of V2 rockets was taking place, became known to British Intelligence in June 1943. On the moonlit night of 17/18 August 1943 Bomber Command despatched 596 aircraft to this distant target. Forty of these aircraft were lost, most of them shot down by nightfighters. About 180 Germans were killed, including some scientists, as well as about 500 foreign workers. The raid resulted in dispersal of the establishment and it was estimated that the rocket programme was set back by about eight weeks. These enlargements of parts of the target were made from photographs taken by photo-reconnaissance aircraft.

PRO ref: AIR 14/3671

The 'Berlin Gerät', a 10 centimetre air interception scanner used in Junkers Ju88s, under examination by an RAF flight lieutenant.

PRO ref: AIR 14/2661

The nose of the Junkers Ju88G-7c was specially adapted to fit the scanner.

PRO ref: AIR 14/2661

The cockpit installation in a Junkers Ju88 nightfighter, showing the control lever for the 'Berlin Gerät' scanner and the cathode ray unit.

PRO ref: AIR 14/2661

The cockpit installation in a Junkers Ju88 nightfighter, with the display unit for the 'Naxos' radar on the left and the display unit for the 'Lichtenstein SN2' on the right.

PRO ref: AIR 14/2661

A daylight attack on V1 flying bomb sites between Flixecourt and Domart-en-Ponthieu, north of Amiens, on 14 January 1944. It was carried out by Boston IIIs of 107 Squadron and the Free French 342 (GB 1/20 Lorraine) Squadron, both based at Hartfordbridge as part of Bomber Command's 2 Group.

PRO ref: AIR 37/334

(*Opposite, top*) A Junkers Ju88 nightfighter fitted with 'Lichtenstein SN2' aerial array for air interception of RAF bombers, together with a blister on top of the cockpit for homing on to H2S, a radar navigational and target location aid introduced into RAF aircraft in early 1943. The Ju88 was also fitted with two 20 mm cannons slanting upwards (known as *Schräge Musik*), intended to destroy a bomber by firing into the belly of the fuselage and undersurfaces of the engines.

PRO ref: AIR 14/2661

A 'Giant Würzburg' radar (centre left) and a 'Wassermann' radar array on its swivelling column (top right) photographed at La Brasserie near Cherbourg. On 16 March 1944 rocket-firing Typhoons attacked one of these huge Wassermann radars at Ostend, with complete success, and the others were then attacked. Poles erected against glider landings can also be seen in this photograph.

PRO ref: AIR 40/1959

(*Opposite*) This excellent photograph of Königsberg in the Baltic was taken from 23,000 feet on 19 February 1944 by a Mosquito PR IX of 540 Squadron, based at Benson in Oxfordshire. Photo-interpreters were able to identify sixteen U-boats and the light cruiser *Köln*, which had been stripped of her armament.

PRO ref: AIR 15/472

A 'Freya' radar (centre left) and the paraboloid dish of a 'Giant Würzburg' radar (centre left) at Cap de la Hève near Le Havre. It was estimated that about a hundred of these radar stations were built by the Germans along the 450 miles of coastline between the Franco-Belgian border and Cap Fréhel in Brittany. Most of these were destroyed by rocket-firing Typhoons and Spitfire fighter-bombers of the 2nd Tactical Air Force before D-Day, 6 June 1944.

PRO ref: AIR 40/1959

A badly damaged 'Würzburg Reise' and signal station at Cap Levy in France photographed on 30 June 1944 after capture by British commandos.

PRO ref: ADM 202/598

A 'Jagdschloss' installation, in which the lower aerial array was of the 'Freya' type, providing a narrow band system, and the upper a 'Fuge 25A' interrogator aerial array. 'Freya', the Nordic Venus, was the name given to a medium-range system which appeared in many forms and was used for area surveillance of approaching bombers.

PRO ref: AIR 14/2661

A 'Wassermann' (chimney) installation at Römö in Denmark, with a rotating aerial array which was broad-band and horizontally polarized. The 'Wassermann' was considered the best of the German long-range early warning systems.

PRO ref: AIR 14/2661

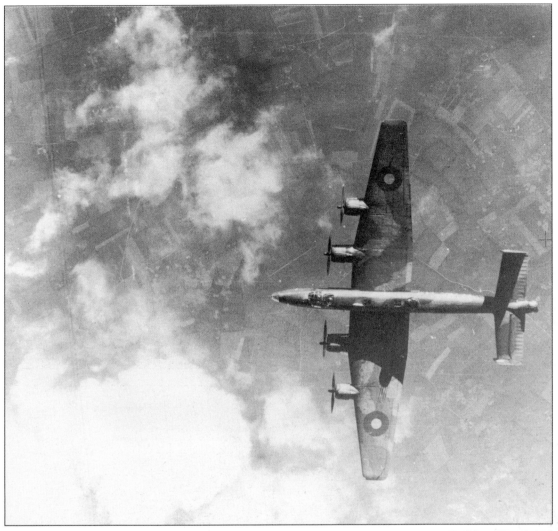

This photograph dated 3 August 1944 was taken from 15,000 feet from a Halifax III of 433 (RCAF) Squadron, based at Skipton-on-Swale in Yorkshire, when over Forêt de Nieppe during a daylight attack against V1 flying bomb stores in northern France. It showed another Halifax below, with the evening sun casting long shadows which showed the effect of the mid-upper turret and its four machine-guns on the port wing.

PRO ref: AIR 14/3647

(*Opposite*) The 'Würzburg Reise' was the most common medium-range radar employed by the Luftwaffe for precision tracking of aircraft until it was neutralized by aluminium foil 'Window' dropped by RAF bombers from mid-1943. This installation had a paraboloid of 30 feet in diameter, to which was fitted a spinning dipole of 600 megacycles per second, a 'Gema' long-range array of 130 megacycles per second, and a 'Fuge 25A' interrogator aerial array on the upper lip of the paraboloid.

PRO ref: AIR 14/2661

A Handley Page Halifax photographed from 19,000 feet during a daylight attack on 12 September 1944 against Münster. The raid was carried out by 119 Halifaxes of Bomber Command's 4 Group and five Lancasters of No. 8 (Pathfinder Force) Group. Extensive damage was caused to the southern part of the city but two Halifaxes failed to return.

PRO ref: AIR 14/3701

(*Overleaf*) This photograph shows a Lancaster 1 (Special) of 617 Squadron scoring a hit on a bridge. The squadron letters YZ and the aircraft letter E can be seen on the original photograph. The PRO document states that this refers to an attack on 14 August 1944, but the squadron bombed Brest harbour on that day. The photograph was probably taken on 4 August 1944, when 617 Squadron attacked a railway bridge at Etaples, dropping 1,000 lb bombs which damaged but did not destroy the bridge.

PRO ref: AIR 14/3647

Small strips of foil, code-named 'Window', being dropped near Gelsenkirchen in the Ruhr during daylight raids by 412 aircraft of Bomber Command against targets in Germany. This foil, which was first dropped during Bomber Command's massive raid against Hamburg on the night of 24/25 July 1943, was designed to disrupt German Würzburg radar. The photograph was taken from a Halifax III of 158 Squadron flown by a Canadian pilot, Flying Officer V.F. Lewis, from its base at Lissett in Yorkshire.

PRO ref: AIR 14/3647

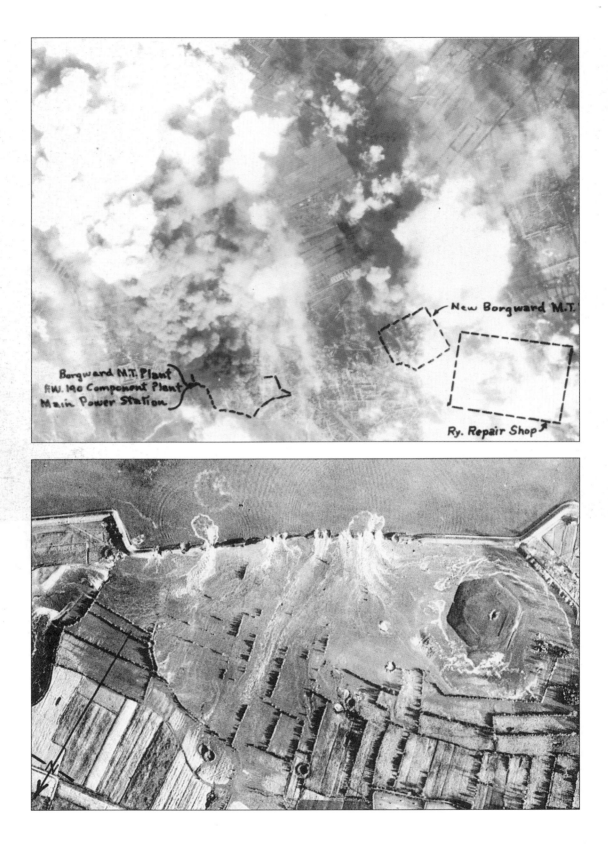

An attack against Flushing in Walcheren took place on 28 October 1944 when German gun positions in the part not flooded by sea water were bombed by 277 aircraft. This photograph was taken from 9,000 feet from a Lancaster of 186 Squadron based at Tuddenham in Suffolk, showing a bomber at lower level with a bomb splash beneath its nose.

PRO ref: AIR 14/3677

(*Opposite, top*) On 12 October 1944 the United States Eighth Air Force dispatched 262 B-17 Flying Fortresses on a daylight attack against Bremen, escorted by 246 P-51 Mustangs and 49 P-47 Thunderbolts. Considerable damage was caused to industrial targets and railway facilities, as shown by the explosions in this annotated photograph.

PRO ref: AIR 37/1231

(*Opposite, bottom*) The sea walls near Flushing in the Dutch island of Walcheren, where strong German forces were holding out and impeding the Allied advance, were breached during an attack by 123 aircraft of Bomber Command on 7 October 1944. As a result of this and other attacks, the inundation of sea water split the island into four parts.

PRO ref: AIR 14/3677

This photograph showing the destruction of a Messerschmitt Bf110 by a Mosquito nightfighter accompanied a report dated November 1944 of the month's activities of Bomber Command's 100 Group. This Group had been formed a year previously for radio counter-measures and other special duties. The Mosquito was engaged on bomber support, patrolling between the targets of Bochum and Ladbergen, when the crew noticed that the German airfield of Münster-Handorf was showing signs of activity. A contact was made 5 miles north-east of the airfield and pursued for twenty minutes. At 2,500 feet the crew were able by using night-glasses to see the German nightfighter above them. It was identified as a Bf110 fitted with drop-tanks, showing a blue-green light underneath. The Mosquito pilot opened fire from 600 yards when dead astern, and the shells were seen to strike the fuselage and wing roots. After three bursts, the enemy aircraft dived vertically through cloud and a violent explosion is seen on the ground shortly afterwards.

PRO ref: AIR 25/782

(*Opposite*) When Field-Marshal Gerd von Rundstedt launched the final effort of the Wehrmacht against the Western Allies in the Ardennes on 16 December 1944, his forces had the advantage of the low cloud and rain which severely restricted the Allied air forces for a week. As soon as the weather began to clear, however, air attacks helped to bring the German advance to a halt and eventually to a retreat. On 26 December 1944 Bomber Command mounted a daylight attack with 294 aircraft against a German troop concentration at St Vith in the Ardennes, where a great battle was in progress. This photograph was taken from 12,000 feet by a Lancaster of 218 Squadron based at Chedburgh in Suffolk.

PRO ref: AIR 14/3663

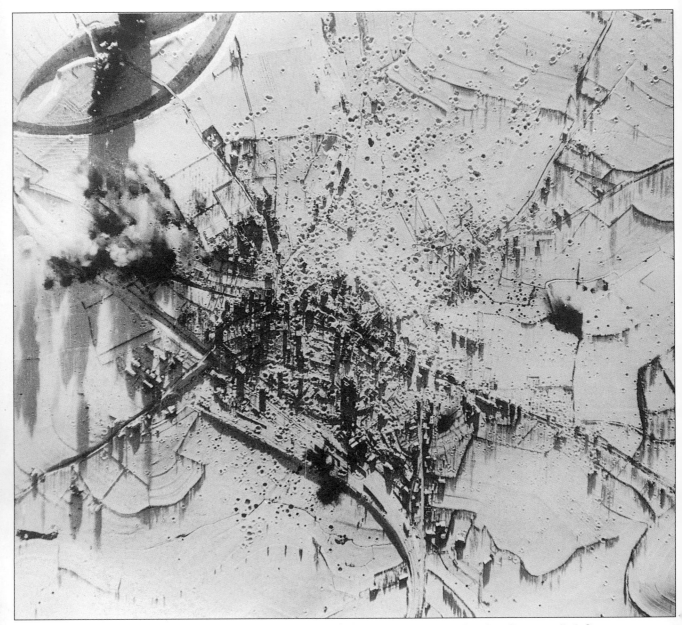

Attacks against the German formations in the Ardennes were carried out by Bomber Command's 2 Group, attached to the 2nd Tactical Air Force. On 5 January 1945 bombs fell on the railway lines in the snow-covered outskirts of St Vith. The centre of the town had been devastated by attacks by Bomber Command.

PRO ref: AIR 37/46

(*Opposite*) This Halifax III, serial MZ465, of 51 Squadron left Snaith in Yorkshire on the evening of 13 January 1945 to participate in an attack by 274 aircraft on Saarbrücken. On the way home after dropping the bombs, the nose of the aircraft was hit by the fin of another Halifax which crossed unexpectedly from starboard. The nose was cut clean off and the navigator and bomb aimer, who were not wearing their clip-on parachute packs, fell to their deaths. Although the propellers were dented, the engines continued to function and the pilot, Flying Officer L. Wilson, was able to bring the damaged aircraft back to England.

PRO ref: AIR 14/1443

An attack by the 2nd Tactical Air Force against the Gestapo headquarters in Shell House, Copenhagen, was planned with the aid of this model prepared by V (Model) Section of the Allied Central Interpretation Unit at Medmenham in Buckinghamshire. The main building was indicated by an arrow in this photograph. In addition, a relief map was constructed for the low-level attack, showing all the main landmarks and with possible obstructions indicated by pins.

PRO ref: AIR 37/46

(*Opposite*) On 17 April 1945 five Mosquitos and eight Mustangs of the 2nd Tactical Air Force attacked the Gestapo headquarters at Odense in the Danish island of Fünen. The centre of the main frontage was destroyed, as shown in this photograph taken by a Mosquito from a film unit which accompanied the bombers and joined in the attack.

PRO ref: AIR 37/46

The attack against the Gestapo headquarters in Copenhagen was carried out on 21 March 1945 by Mosquito IVs of 21 Squadron, 464 (RAAF) Squadron and 487 (RNZAF) Squadron. The building was gutted, as shown in this photograph taken by the Danish Underground Movement, and twenty-six members of the Gestapo were killed. Very sadly there was also a tragedy – in the smoke and confusion, some of the bombs fell on a nearby school and resulted in many casualties to the schoolchildren.

PRO ref: AIR 37/46

This photograph, taken from 12,000 feet on 25 April 1945 during a daylight attack against coastal batteries on the German island of Wangerooge on the approaches to Bremen and Wilhelmshaven, illustrated the dangers of congestion, with one Lancaster immediately above another. Bomber Command despatched 482 aircraft on this raid. Seven bombers were lost, six of them as a result of collisions.

PRO ref: AIR 14/3647

The 12,000 lb 'Tallboy' bomb in flight. It was developed by the scientist Barnes Wallis and first dropped by 617 Squadron during the night of 8/9 June 1944 on a railway tunnel near Saumur, to prevent a German Panzer unit moving up to the battle area in Normandy. These bombs also destroyed the battleship *Tirpitz* at Tromsö in Norway on 12 November 1944.

PRO ref: AIR 14/3647

The 22,000 lb 'Grand Slam' bomb being dropped by a Lancaster I (Special) of 617 Squadron. This huge bomb was also developed by the scientist Barnes Wallis and first dropped by 617 Squadron on 14 March 1945 on the viaduct at Bielefeld in Germany.

PRO ref: AIR 14/3647

This photograph was taken on 12 March 1945 from a Lancaster of 166 Squadron, based at Kirmington in Lincolnshire and flown by Squadron Leader R. Waters, during a daylight raid on Dortmund. The bomb load consisted of a 4,000 lb blast bomb (known as a 'blockbuster' or 'cookie') as well as twelve 500 lb and four 250 lb bombs. Bomber Command despatched 1,108 aircraft to this target, which was completely covered by cloud but accurately marked by the Pathfinder Force. Two Lancasters were lost, but enormous destruction was caused to the centre and south of the city.

PRO ref: AIR 14/3647

The headquarters staff of Bomber Command's 2 Group marked the end of the Second World War in Europe, VE Day on 8 May 1945, with a parade in an open square in Brussels. The men and women were addressed by their Air Officer Commanding, Air Vice-Marshal Basil E. Embry CBE DSO DFC. As a Wing Commander with 107 Squadron, Embry had been shot down over France on 27 May 1940. He escaped from his German captors and after many adventures reached Gibraltar and was brought back to England by the Royal Navy.

PRO ref: AIR 37/46

These captured German cameras were photographed by the RAF on 21 July 1945. From left to right, the camera types were Rb75/30, Rb50/30 and Rb20/30. Rb was short for *Rehenbilder* (series pictures), while the next two figures denoted the focal length of the lens in centimetres. The Rb75 lens probably had a telephoto element and was thus somewhat shorter than 75 cm. The 30 represented the format size of the photographs, 30 cm by 30 cm, contained in the standard magazine held by the airman. The cameras produced excellent results but their size and weight limited their use in the very high-level photography required when defending fighters became capable of reaching very high altitudes.

PRO ref: AIR 37/1441

D-DAY AND BEYOND

A close-up of beach obstacles along the French coast, exposed at low tide, photographed from very low level. These defences consisted of stakes to which shells were attached and platforms with ramps on which Teller mines were fixed, each mine being about 13 inches in diameter and containing over 11½ lb of TNT.

PRO ref: AIR 40/1959

(*Opposite*) Horsa gliders under tow by Halifaxes and Stirlings, while the crews were under training before D-Day.

PRO ref: AIR 37/1231

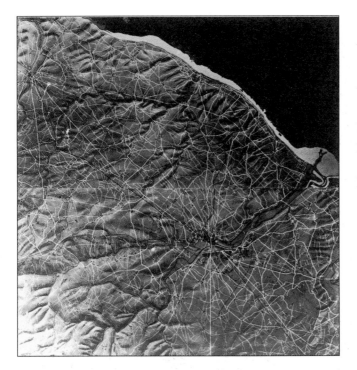

A model relief map on a scale of 1:25,000 of the country around Caen and Bayeux in Normandy, made by V (Model) Section of the Allied Central Interpretation Unit at Medmenham in Buckinghamshire preparatory to D-Day. It was constructed from vertical and oblique photographs taken by photo-reconnaissance aircraft and then studied by W (Photogrammetric) Section. This model included the Gold Area (where the British 50th Group landed), the Sword Area (where the 3rd Canadian Division Group landed) and the Juno Area (where the British 3rd Division Group landed).

PRO ref: AIR 40/1959

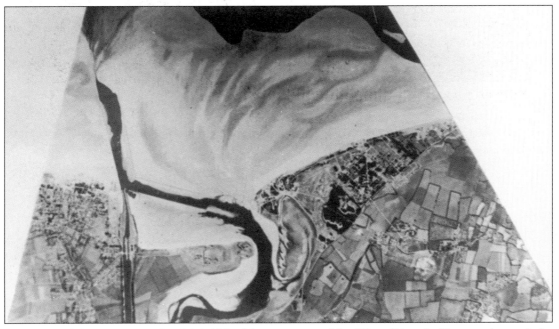

A model relief map on a scale of 1:5,000 of the entrance of the River Dives in Normandy, made by V (Model) Section of the Allied Central Interpretation Unit. These models were made by volunteer artists, architects and sculptors in the new RAF trade of 'Pattern-Makers, Architectural'. Each model was made from rubberized material which could be rolled up for ease of transport.

PRO ref: AIR 40/1959

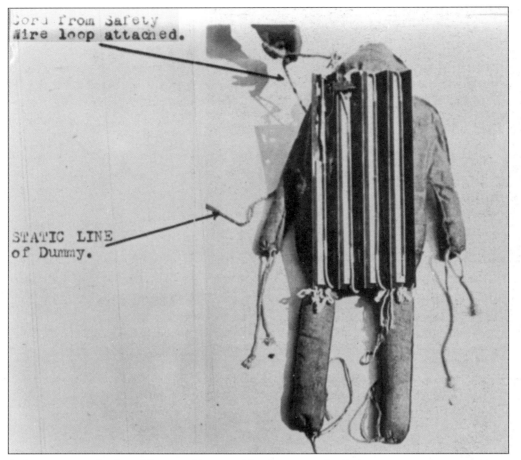

A dummy parachutist with a machine-gun simulator attached.

PRO ref: AIR 24/281

The Airspeed Horsa was Britain's first troop-carrying glider to be employed on operational work. It was made in wood, mainly by furniture manufacturers, and the parts were assembled on RAF airfields. It carried two pilots of the Army's Glider Pilot Regiment and about twenty-five troops with their arms. This prototype, serial DG597, was first flown on 12 September 1941 and was followed by 3,655 production aircraft. Gliders were towed by RAF aircraft and released some distance from their targets so that they could approach silently. The Horsa was also used widely by the USAAF for US airborne troops.

PRO ref: SUPP 9/1

(*Opposite*) The first airborne assault troops to arrive in Normandy on D-Day were from the 2nd Battalion, Oxfordshire and Buckinghamshire Light Infantry, together with men from the Royal Engineers, medical staff and a liaison officer from the 7th Parachute Battalion. They were transported in six Horsa gliders flown by men of the Glider Pilot Regiment and towed by six Halifaxes of 298 and 644 Squadrons based at Tarrant Rushton in Dorset. Their objective was to capture intact two bridges, over the River Orne and the Caen canal. This photograph shows the three gliders which landed exactly on target at 00.16 hours beside the bridge over the Caen canal. Nearest the bridge is Horsa No. 91 flown by Staff Sergeant James Wallwork. A few yards away is Horsa No. 93 flown by Staff Sergeant Geoffrey Barkway, with lastly, Horsa No. 92 flown by Staff Sergeant Oliver Boland. The troops captured the bridge after a stiff fight. Two of the other gliders landed beside the River Orne bridge and captured it. The troops then held the two bridges against German counter-attacks until reinforcements arrived. The bridge over the Caen canal was later renamed the Pegasus Bridge, after the insignia of the Glider Pilot Regiment.

PRO ref: DEFE 2/429

On 10 June 1944 the first airfield in Normandy was completed at Ste Croix-sur-Mer, about 2 miles inland from Gold Beach. Four of the RAF's Servicing Commandos and Construction Wings had come ashore three days previously. The men first dug trenches for themselves as protection from shellfire and then set to work with excavators, bulldozers and powered rollers. The men in this photograph are laying steel wire mesh to construct the runway.

PRO ref: DEFE 2/502

The Mulberry harbour at Arromanches in the British Gold area, photographed on 2 October 1944. It consisted of blockships and prefabricated concrete caissons forming breakwaters and pier units.

PRO ref: DEFE 2/499

Unloading operations on the beach at Vierville in the American sector. This mosaic was constructed from several vertical photographs taken as a line overlap.

PRO ref: AIR 37/1231

Prefabricated sections of the artificial 'Mulberry' harbours being marshalled off the southern coast of England before being towed to Normandy.

PRO ref: AIR 37/1231

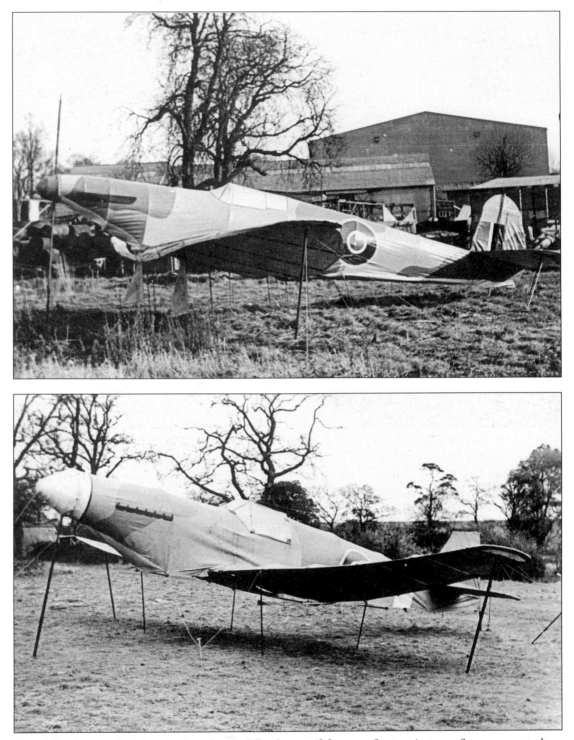

A mobile dummy Spitfire (top) and a mobile dummy Mustang (bottom), two of many erected on dummy airfields to deceive unwary airmen of the Luftwaffe.

PRO ref: AIR 20/4349

The RAF's Group Control Centre in Normandy received signals from the RAF's Wireless Observer Units regarding the course, speed and altitude of approaching enemy aircraft. These were passed to the Senior Controller who alerted fighter squadrons which were kept at readiness to intercept any hostile visitors.

PRO ref: DEFE 2/502

This photograph, taken soon after D-Day, showed Corporal Lydia Alford of the WAAF helping a wounded soldier into an RAF Dakota which was operating as an air ambulance. The RAF's Group M (Medical) was open to women and included the function of nursing orderly.

MoD ref: CL114

The whole of the Siegfried Line on the frontier of Germany was photographed during August 1944, in preparation for the Allied advance. The photographs were annotated to show defence positions.

PRO ref: AIR 37/1231

(*Opposite*) RAF Brize Norton, near Witney in Oxfordshire, was opened for flying training in 1937 and later became a Heavy Glider Conversion Unit. This photograph was taken on 20 March 1951 and showed the two runways, both of 2,000 yards.

PRO ref: AIR 14/3702

Horsa gliders lined up at Brize Norton in Oxfordshire in September 1944, flanked by their tugs, Armstrong Whitworth Albemarles of 296 and 297 Squadrons. These gliders were among the first to descend on Arnhem on 17 September 1944 on operation 'Market', the airborne attempt to capture bridges over the Rhine behind the German lines and establish a bridgehead which the advancing British 2nd Army was to secure under operation 'Garden'.

PRO ref: AIR 14/3650

The main landing zone west of Arnhem, littered with gliders. All the pilots were from the Army's Glider Pilot Regiment.

PRO ref: AIR 14/3650

Paratroops of the British 1st Parachute Brigade being dropped near Arnhem from C-47 Dakotas of the United States IX Troop Carrier Command.

PRO ref: AIR 14/3650

Troops moving into action at Arnhem, with a Hamilcar glider in the foreground.

PRO ref: AIR 14/3650

A General Aircraft Hamilcar glider after landing at Arnhem on 17 September 1944. This was the largest glider employed by the British during the war, its main purpose being to carry freight such as light tanks to landing zones. The nose was hinged so that vehicles could be driven in and out.

PRO ref: AIR 14/3650

Troops unloading from a Hamilcar glider at Arnhem.

PRO ref: AIR 14/3650

Supplies being dropped by Stirlings over Arnhem.

PRO ref: AIR 14/3650

Wrecked German vehicles on the northern end of the Arnhem bridge. This was the scene of much bitter fighting before the Germans finally overcame the British airborne forces on 21 September 1944.

PRO ref: AIR 14/3650

Men of the RAF Regiment with German trophies captured during a reconnaissance in the forward areas.

MoD ref: CL408

The bridge over the Rhine at Remagen, south of Cologne, was unexpectedly captured by the US 27th Armoured Infantry on 7 March 1945, in spite of an attempt by the Germans to dynamite it. American troops were able to swarm across it and establish their main bridgehead in Germany. The bridge collapsed about two weeks later but by that time pontoon bridges had been built. This photograph was taken by an aircraft of the United States Eighth Air Force.

PRO ref: AIR 37/1231

This Focke-Achgelis Fa223-E Drache (Kite) helicopter, experimental number V-14, was captured by the US Army in May 1945 from *Luft-Transportstaffel 40* at Ainring in Austria. It was then flown by the Luftwaffe crew to the Airborne Forces Experimental Establishment at RAF Beaulieu in Hampshire, where it underwent experiments during the following September and October. However, it was wrecked in an accident before complete evaluation for such duties as anti-submarine, reconnaissance, air/sea rescue, transport and training.

PRO ref: AVIA 21/238

THE FORGOTTEN WAR

RAF Dum-Dum was one of the main bases of the Eastern Air Command in the war against the Japanese in Burma and for flying supplies over the 'hump' to Kunming in China. Aircraft on the airfield when this photograph was taken included Douglas C-47 Dakotas, Lockheed P-38 Lightnings, Lockheed Hudsons, North American Mitchells, Hawker Hurricanes, de Havilland Mosquitos and de Havilland Rapides.

PRO ref: AIR 23/4292

This reconnaissance photograph was taken after the Japanese conquest of Burma in 1942, showing a bridge under construction at Mawle on the Maw river, near the Chin Hills on the approaches to India.

PRO ref: AIR 23/4292

The completed bridge ten days later.

PRO ref: AIR 23/4292

Stationary trucks on the railway line between Mandalay and Monya, being attacked on 18 July 1943 with cannon and machine-gun fire by Beaufighter VIs of 27 Squadron based at Agartala in India.

PRO ref: AIR 23/4292

The paddle steamer *Maha*, under Japanese control, during an attack by RAF Beaufighters on 1 October 1943 when near Alon on the Chindwin river in Burma.

PRO ref: AIR 23/4292

This publicity photograph showed RAF armourers loading belts of cannon shells into the wings of a Hurricane engaged on close support for the 14th Army on the Burma front.

PRO ref: AIR 23/4291

Incendiaries falling towards Ngazaunghpet on the Kaladan river at the junction of the Praing Chaung, north of Akyab in Burma, when the village was occupied by Japanese forces.

PRO ref: AIR 23/4292

This Spitfire PR XI, serial PA935, was on the strength of 681 Squadron, which was based in India until moving to Mingaladon near Rangoon on 25 May 1945. The squadron was equipped with this mark of aircraft from September 1943 to April 1946. Unarmed and painted in special 'PR blue', these Spitfires were employed on long-distance photo-reconnaissance work over Japanese positions in Burma.

PRO ref: AIR 23/4291

Ground crews of a cannon-firing Spitfire squadron setting up their mobile workshop on a new airstrip in central Burma during the advance of the British 14th Army in the final stages of the war. The equipment was landed by air while the ground crews and administrative personnel were brought in by motor transport. A minor monsoon was in progress when this photograph was taken.

PRO ref: AIR 23/4291

This Douglas C-47 Dakota was photographed arriving at an airstrip in central Burma, bringing supplies and mail for the Army and the RAF. The use of this highly reliable aircraft revolutionized warfare in the Far East by enabling ground forces to operate in remote areas, either by landing on airstrips or dropping supplies.

PRO ref: AIR 23/4291

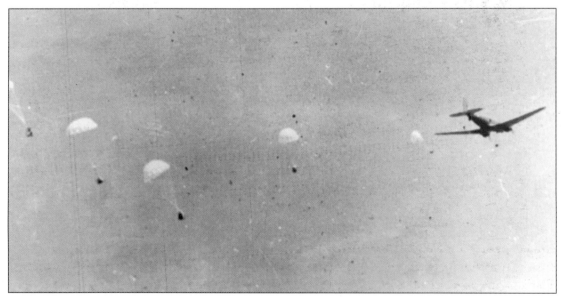

A C-47 Dakota dropping supplies to the advancing troops of the 14th Army in central Burma.

PRO ref: AIR 23/4291

In December 1944, when based at Redhill Lake in India and engaged primarily on patrols with Consolidated Catalinas over the Bay of Bengal, 240 Squadron was given the additional task of dropping supplies and agents behind Japanese positions in the Dutch East Indies. During 11 and 12 January 1945 Catalina P, flown by the commanding officer, Wing Commander B.A.C. Wood, took part in trials when canisters and live parachute drops were made from the gun blisters in the fuselage. A portable table was built for each blister, with a chute fitted over the rear hatch, to be mounted over the dropping zone.

PRO ref: AIR 27/1461

The first tests were made on 11 January 1945 in collaboration with Lieutenant-Colonel Lucius O. Rucker of the US Army. A site was chosen about 9 miles from Redhill Lake. On the first run, a canister of about 120 lb was dropped through the hole in the port blister. Rucker dropped on the second run, using a static line, and landed safely. Although the site appeared to be deserted, hundreds of Indians suddenly appeared to watch the proceedings. Other successful trials took place the following day.

PRO ref: AIR 27/1461

On 24 March 1945 forty-three RAF Liberators of Eastern Air Command's Strategic Air Force set off from India to bomb Japanese rolling stock and supply dumps in a dispersal area at Pa-Auk, near Moulmein in Burma. They were escorted by twenty-four P-51 Mustang long-distance fighters of the United States Tenth Air Force.

PRO ref: AIR 23/4292

The Liberators found their objectives and delivered devastating attacks. All aircraft returned safely.
PRO ref: AIR 23/4292

The Japanese headquarters at Meiktila in central Burma, destroyed by RAF bombers of Eastern Air Command. The town was recaptured by the British at the end of February 1945. Flying Officer James Davie, the Armaments Officer of an RAF Servicing Commando Unit, was photographed examining the damage.

PRO ref: AIR 23/4292

On 15 June 1945 eight Liberator VIs of 355 Squadron took off from Salbani in India to attack the Japanese tanker *Toho Maru* of 10,238 tons near the island of Koh Samoi in the Gulf of Siam. Six aircraft returned early owing to monsoon weather but the remaining two carried on and found their target. Each Liberator attacked with six 500 lb medium-capacity bombs, straddling the vessel. One bomb hit the stern, setting her on fire, and she sank. This photograph was taken at an early stage of the attack.

PRO ref: AIR 23/4292

This photograph was taken from 1,500 feet on 8 June 1945 when a Liberator VI of 159 Squadron, flown by Squadron leader T.W. Watson, was one of eight aircraft which dropped showers of 100 lb fragmentation bombs on a Japanese troop concentration and stores dump at Bilin in the south-west of Burma. The squadron was part of the RAF's 231 Group and was based at Digri in India.

PRO ref: AIR 23/4292

This photograph of shattered oil tanks at Rangoon was taken from 500 feet on 3 May 1945 by a Liberator VI of 159 Squadron flown from Digri in India by Pilot Officer R. Lee. The purpose of the flight was to drop food and medical supplies to Allied prisoners-of-war in the central jail nearby. The prisoners rushed out and collected the supplies. The crew of the Liberator noted that the roofs of the jail were painted with notices: 'JAPS GONE', 'BRITISH HERE', 'JAPS EVACUATED', 'DON'T PRANG RANGOON', 'EXTRACT DIGIT'. In fact the Japanese had departed on 25 April and the crew of an RAF Mosquito had landed at the nearby airfield of Mingaladon on 2 May. The British 26th Division entered Rangoon on the day this photograph was taken, and the ordeal of the prisoners was over.

PRO ref: AIR 23/4307

This two-span bridge at Chumphon near the eastern coast of the Kra peninsula of Siam (Thailand), carrying the railway line to Singapore, was bombed by RAF Liberators of Eastern Air Command's Strategic Air Force on 22 May 1945. The photograph showed that a steel girder span had crashed into the river while a bomb was exploding at the end of the bridge.

PRO ref: AIR 23/4307

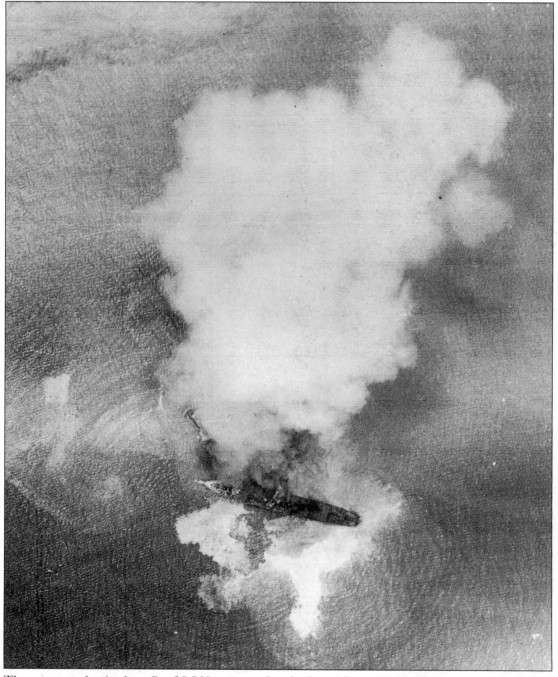

The steam yacht *Angthong-Go* of 2,760 tons was bombed on 1 June 1945 by Liberators of the RAF's 231 Group, Eastern Air Command, when off the village of Satahib in the Gulf of Siam. The vessel, which was being used by the Japanese as a submarine depot ship, sank in about four minutes. Apparently there were no survivors since the Japanese records stated that its loss occurred on 4 June 1945, when presumably it was given up as lost.

PRO ref: AIR 23/4292

The main bridge at Kanchanaburi over the river Khwae in Siam, part of the Burma–Siam railway which was built in appalling conditions by forced labour under Japanese control, was destroyed when twenty Liberators of the RAF's 231 Group, Eastern Air Command, bombed it on 24 June 1945. Eventually three spans were demolished in the attack, although only one span had been destroyed when this photograph was taken. In addition, a bypass bridge outside this photograph was destroyed in the attack.

PRO ref: AIR 23/4292

The blast of the atom bomb which was dropped on Hiroshima on 6 August 1945 killed about 78,000 people and demolished up to 90,000 buildings within an area of 4 square miles. Only a few reinforced concrete buildings were left standing.

PRO ref: CAB 80/99

INDEX